Fortunate Daughter

Fortunate Daughter

A Memoir of Reconciliation

ROSIE MCMAHAN

She Writes Press, a BookSparks imprint
A Division of SparkPointStudio, LLC.

Published 2021
Printed in the United States of America

Print ISBN: 978-1-64742-024-6
E-ISBN: 978-1-64742-025-3
Library of Congress Control Number: 2020921761

For information, address:
She Writes Press
1569 Solano Ave #546
Berkeley, CA 94707

She Writes Press is a division of SparkPoint Studio, LLC.
All company and/or product names may be trade names, logos, trademarks, and/or registered trademarks and are the property of their respective owners.

Names and identifying characteristics have been changed to protect the privacy of certain individuals.

As many as one in three girls and one in seven boys will be sexually abused at some point in their childhood. The people who sexually abuse children are most often people they know, and frequently people they care about.

From http://www.stopitnow.org/csa fact who abuse

■—·—·—■

Victims of childhood sexual assault are two to eleven times more likely to experience revictimization in adulthood.

From T. Messman-Moore and P. Long, "The Role of Childhood Sexual Abuse Sequelae in the Sexual Revictimization Of Women: An Empirical Review and Theoretical Reformulation," *Clinical Psychology Review 23* (2003), 537–71.

In my twin bed, I faced the wall
the one connecting my bedroom to my parents.
In the shadowy silence,
I would gaze at the wallpaper
before falling asleep,
the same wallpaper that I chose and helped to put up;
violet, blossoming roses,
petals opening in various stages of growth,
surrounded by pea-green leaves.
At night, I would lie still,
pretending I was a tiny person
climbing in and out of the showy folds,
comforted by their presence
as I waited for my Daddy.

CONTENTS

PART ONE

"The way to right wrongs is to turn the light of truth upon them."
—Ida Wells

PART TWO

*"When you write, you illuminate what's hidden,
and that's a political act."*—Grace Paley

PART THREE

*"Where there is reconciliation, Stephen says,
there must have been a sundering."* —James Joyce

PROLOGUE

My father died on January 11, 2011, a few months and many years after I got up the courage to ask him about how he understood the past and his ability to hurt me, my siblings, and my mother the way he did. This was almost twenty-five years after I had met with both my parents for the final time with a therapist, marking a long process of reconciliation.

During those years, there had been many moments he could have told me something to help me understand where his capacity to do harm began. Maybe it would have made a difference earlier in my life. In his life, too. I don't know. I do know that my father hated excuses, having been raised during a time when the reasons for one's mistakes didn't matter.

I recall sitting with him in my parent's kitchen in Somerville. The air was crisp on a beautiful autumn day and my mother had gone out to run errands. As I sipped my coffee, I acted a whole lot calmer than I felt. My guess is he did, too.

He started this way. "Do you remember Gramma ever talking about Sinclair Connelly?" I realized he was about to tell me something he never had. And that it wouldn't be a straight line. Never was with my dad.

"Sinclair was something," he said and stared out the back window, but appeared to be looking at something much farther away. He then pointed. "That tree is right pretty every year at this time. See how the yella sweet-talks the blue?" I cocked my head to see where he aimed his finger and thought for a second about complementary colors. Blue and yellow. Red and cyan. Green and magenta. I wondered if my dad had ever wanted to be an artist. If so, had it ever been possible for him to imagine how to make that real in his life? Growing up, I remember how he would often draw attention to beautiful patterns that would appear in the natural world. It was all I could do to hold my coffee mug steady, letting the creamy, sweet smell waft against my cheeks.

"I was told to walk to their house, it weren't more than a few miles, to do work, deliver messages, whatever was needed." He paused. "I felt so proud of myself. I couldn't have been more than seven. I also liked being gone for hours at a stretch. Richard, their son, he was about one year older than me at the time. He's the one who told me, 'You gots to sleep naked in this here house while you're here.' I thought it was strange, but I did as I was told. You wouldn't think about disobeying adults back then. And you didn't want nothing coming back to your kin, either."

A wave of sorrow washed over me, but I didn't speak or move.

"And I slept naked between Sinclair and their son, Richard." He looked down after the words left his mouth, and I remembered that this wasn't the first time I had attempted to get him to talk. There was that night when I was sixteen, needing to get away and having spent the whole summer with his mother, Gramma.

We had taken a walk up to the top of Chestnut Mountain. Suddenly, there was the sound of a whippoorwill, the well-known three parts: "WHIP-poor-WEEA," with a rising last note and first and last syllables accented. Dad and I looked toward a log at the edge of the small clearing, and neither of us spoke. He took out a flashlight and shined it toward the direction of the sound. Light reflected from the corneas of two pairs of eyes much closer to the ground than I anticipated.

"They must be nesting," he said. "They use the light of the moon in their courtship with one another."

Prologue

"That call is unusual. I can't imagine being raised around that noise and ever wanting to leave it."

"Well, they weren't the only sounds I heard."

"What do you mean?"

Ever quick to change the subject, he said, "You seem like you've enjoyed being here."

"It's been good, but I don't like how Gramma pretends to be all good and then judges everybody so harshly, especially Mom." I wanted to talk more about other sounds that made him leave his home, maybe the sounds that taught him to do what he did.

I asked, "Why'd you leave North Carolina if you love it so much? It seems like the place you're most yourself."

"I had to; there was nothing for me to do here to make a living. And my dad was a hard man to be around."

"But you seem happier when you're here."

"In some ways." He stretched his legs out and leaned back toward the heavens. "It's always easier being somewhere that you don't have to work. There's no stress. Like a lot of men, I can be a good man for a little while."

I blurted out, "Do you think you did bad things to Mom and us kids because of how you were raised?" and then despaired that my question sounded accusatory. We were talking to one another honestly. I wasn't afraid, and he wasn't antagonistic.

"Nah. We make our own decisions despite what happens to us. My brothers are good examples. They didn't get raised no differently than me," he said and then paused as if to say something else but didn't. Instead, he put his head in his hands like a warrior taking a rest.

"Maybe we're not the only ones deciding," I said. "You did some bad things to us. You do know that?"

"I do."

"I worried before coming here, back to where you were born and raised, that I was broken forever."

Fortunate Daughter

"I was worried I might have broken you."

"For what you did?"

"That, and for who I was."

The words shot like an arrow, from a quiver of wisdom: what everyone in my family would love to hear, finally spoken.

How defeated he seemed then, I now thought, sitting there in the kitchen almost thirty years later. How defeated he seemed now. Everything around us got quiet; I felt the house and all the furnishings lean in and listen. "It went on for years," he said.

"What did they do?" I asked, not certain if I really wanted to know.

"They molested me. Touched me, kissed me. I never liked it, it felt yucky. It made me feel bad, partly 'cuz it made me feel good."

"You never told anyone?" I asked, but knew what his answer would be.

"Nope, kids didn't tell on adults, ever. We'd were too afraid we'd get in worse trouble for telling."

He looked at me. "It wasn't until going through treatment that I said a word to anyone. The only other person besides you who knows is your mother."

And with that, something set loose in me. Dad was not who I thought he was. And I felt myself became someone else, too. I didn't know who we were, not to ourselves or to one another or the world. A part of me unfastened, and I felt more able to see the heart of the matter. Listening to his story, something I couldn't have imagined as possible, let alone helpful, created more space for mending what was broken in me. And I remain unbroken now. We did something special, my whole family and I, that allowed us to heal and not just be identified as defeated. That is my hope in writing all this down and handing these pages to you. That you, too, in whatever ways you need, can do the special thing that will heal the broken parts in you.

PART ONE

Molest: from Old French *molester* or Latin *molestare* 'annoy,' from *molestus* 'troublesome.'

■ — ·— ■

"Child maltreatment is the abuse and neglect that occurs to children under 18 years of age. It includes all types of physical and emotional ill-treatment, sexual abuse, neglect, negligence, and commercial or other exploitation, which results in actual or potential harm to the child's health, survival, development, or dignity in the context of a relationship of responsibility, trust, or power."

—World Health Organization

■ — ·— ■

"The way to right wrongs is to turn the light of truth upon them."

—Ida Wells

1956

No Meat Without the Bone

My parents met and fell in love in 1956, the same year Rosa Parks quietly but firmly took a seat at the front of the bus, Dwight D. Eisenhower was re-elected president of the United States, and Elvis Presley made his first appearance on *The Ed Sullivan Show*. That year, a gallon of gas cost twenty-three cents, the polio vaccine developed by Jonas Salk was made available to the public, Play-Doh was introduced to the world, and Jackson Pollack died in a car crash.

This part of the story isn't mine, at least not in the sense that I experienced it. But I include it because it shaped me as much as anything, maybe more so. What's here, gathered mostly from my mom, reveals more about what I don't know. And that's important, too. For all of us. These people we call our parents. We know them, and we don't know them. For better. For worse.

My mother was a Registered Nurse and lieutenant, working on a locked unit for Korean War vets at the Philadelphia Naval Hospital. At twenty-six years old, she was still single, though she was the oldest in a first-generation Italian family where girls grew up and got married out of high school. It has taken me many years and a lot of growing up to realize how much my mother worried she might never meet someone right. She carried a feeling of isolation and loneliness because of not fitting into a category that was easily understood.

Fortunate Daughter

Proud and Italian, but aware that her ethnic group did not support her aspirations to become a nurse. Educated and professionally ambitious, but yearning to settle down and have a family. A teacher and supervisor, yet easily frightened and self-doubting. Assuming her chances might improve if she lived closer to her Boston home, my mother requested a transfer back east from California.

A small, pretty woman with dark brown eyes and a thin waist, she was walking down the hall one afternoon in her dress blues when she approached my father, then a corpsman working at the front desk. It was her job to get the daily report on the patients, veterans of the Korean War, and introduced herself to the man who would become my father.

My father, wearing an entirely white uniform, had been sitting at the front desk, hunched forward, with his bony elbow resting on his knee and chin in hand. Handsome with a full head of black hair, my father was tall and skinny as a flagpole. The oldest of seven children raised in the mountains of North Carolina by Baptist parents of Scotch-Irish descent, he was obviously younger than she by at least a few years. Yet he was completely at ease in his surroundings. All the nurses relied on the corpsmen for safety, but my father was called upon more than any of the others when a patient got out of control. Rumor had it that he was every nurse's dream, even though the older staff cautioned my mother more than once that he could also speak out of turn and be sassy.

She was curious to find out for herself.

That weekend, when everyone went to the enlisted club, she would go to the Officer's Club and seek out my father again, despite the rule that forbade her from romantic involvement with staff below her rank. It was a rule that wasn't widely observed, and my father didn't seem to object to breaking it, either.

One night, as they parted from one another, my father hung back and leaned against her black car, lighting up a cigarette.

No Meat Without the Bone

"This sure is a pretty Chrysler you got, Miss Rose. Not nearly as pretty as you, though."

She blushed and covered her mouth to hide a smile. "Are all southern men as gallant as you?"

"Can't say as I know. But I'd love to take a drive down to Atlantic City and walk on the boardwalk over the W. W. Memorial Bridge with you."

Only a few months passed before my father proposed as they sat in a local diner for a late supper.

"I knew you were the one for me the first moment I laid on eyes on you, Miss Rose." He gave her knee a gentle squeeze. "Except, I can't rightly figure out why you never order more food."

He'd ordered two meals for himself, heavy on the meat and potatoes. She looked down at her half-eaten buttered corn muffin, then pushed it away. "I don't understand how a man who eats so much stays as thin as you."

"How many times have you told me that you always wanted to live on a farm?" my father asked. "And who cares about our religious differences? I've always wanted to be a Catholic. Even after being 'saved,' I knew I would convert someday. We could make a nice life for ourselves, back where I come from. I know all about the work it takes to make it happen."

She said no that night, but he was persistent. Unlike any man my mother had ever dated, he listened to her when she spoke, seeming to want to understand her, and he was modest, almost too much so. Weeks went by and she continued to put him off because the practical concerns about their differences seemed too great to overcome. I've thought a great deal about what made him so certain that she was the one for him. True love? Destiny? Escape from the tyranny of rural North Carolina?

They married in July 1958 at a church in Medford, Massachusetts, named after Pope Clement of Rome, a saint recognized by the anchor at his side—presumably the one he was tied to before getting thrown from a boat into the Black Sea for his attempt to undermine the king of France. Both of my mother's sisters were married in this same church, but unlike my mother, they'd chosen men who were Catholic and Italian.

At the top of the granite stairs, my parents paused for a moment before exiting the large entranceway as heavy, cold raindrops poured down from the skies.

"It's raining buckets, Ned," my mother whispered to my father, clutching his right hand, feeling her engagement ring rub against his thin gold wedding band. "God help us!"

My father held a large black umbrella over both of them and pulled on her arm as if to make a run for it, but she hesitated.

"You won't get wet with me," he said, and threw his jacket over her shoulders to keep the handwoven satin gown dry.

What follows are letters that my father sent my mother when they were separated, immediately following their honeymoon. I didn't find them, I didn't even know they existed, until after both my parents died. Hidden away in my mother's closet. They reflect a time in their relationship to one another that I sensed had existed but didn't know for certain. They were both still in the Navy and obliged to finish their assignments before they could be stationed somewhere together. My father was nineteen years old.

July 28, 1958
I can see you right now, standing there at the airport waving good-bye. I had a kind of feeling of hope I don't have anymore. But one I will have when we are together again. Seems a bigger part of me was staying there with you. A part that I am just finding out this past week. It is now the bigger part of my life. It is the happiness, the beauty, the warmth, it's just everything. I'm not going to feel right until we are together again.

No Meat Without the Bone

July 29, 1958
I missed you last night. Took me a long time to go to sleep. I kept thinking about you. Oh, I love you. I do. I miss you all the time, especially right now as I write you this letter. Everything is gone without you.

August 4, 1958
You are more than likely writing me. There are no words for some things. Anyway, we are both probably going to feel like this until we are together again.

August 7, 1958
Received a letter from you today. Really enjoyed hearing from you. When I read your letter, I want even more to be with you . . . The nights are very pretty lately. They, like just about everything, remind me of you and my love for you.

August 11, 1958
Don't know how long I can take this not seeing you. Seems everything just crumbles when we have to part. But someday things will be alright. I wonder if you are sleeping now. Will be glad when we are both out of the Navy. Then we can start making some definite plans. I do hope that you are soon pregnant. Whatever will be, will be.

August 14, 1958
Things will be much better as soon as you get out of the Navy. Then we will be able to spend all our time together. Hot dog.

August 22, 1958
Went to the 6:30 a.m. Mass this morning. Seems very strange, you not being by my side. Course we are both praying to the same God. Who hears and answers our prayers. About all for now. I love you. I love you. I do. That's a fact.

Fortunate Daughter

August 29, 1958
Dearest, I better write you. First off, I love you. I really do.
And gosh if something don't hurry and turn out so we can be
together. I don't know what we're going to do . . .

My parents assumed that after you got married, you got pregnant. But a few years passed and that didn't happen, and they didn't know what to do. They had made the decision to live in my mother's hometown, and she went to her doctor for tests. None of these included my father. If a couple couldn't get pregnant, the woman was assumed to be the source of the problem.

Her doctor, a middle-aged Italian man who'd been practicing medicine since 1945, finally said, "I can do nothing more for you, Rosaria."

"Do you think Ned and I should stop trying?"

"This matter is not my concern. It's for you and your husband to decide. I know a woman. She wants to give her unborn baby up for adoption," he told her.

My mother held her breath. "What do you mean?"

"She's a very sad lady. She has one child and cannot take care of another. The baby is due in a few months. The end of September, I think. I don't remember exactly. But you have to meet her. Are you interested?"

"Of course."

She sat down slowly. Was it possible she would have a child? And so suddenly? Her father taught her that things happen for a reason, always for a reason. That God gives you only what you can manage. That people with difficulties are stronger, chosen in fact because of their power and made stronger through their effort to cope. Was she strong enough to become a mother in this way?

"I will make the arrangements," the doctor said. "I know a lawyer. He helps me out with this sort of thing. Don't tell anyone but your husband. Do you understand?"

No Meat Without the Bone

My mother, overjoyed at the possibility that her dream might come true, simply said, "I understand."

My mother went alone the day of the meeting. I don't know why, but I assume my father was working. It was muggy, and a harbor breeze blew in the window of her car as she sat cleaning out her purse, watching for a pregnant stranger to come along and decide her fate. Finally, she left her car and went inside the office building in Davis Square, where the meeting was to take place. As soon as she entered the lobby, she locked eyes with a tired-looking woman, arms folded across a huge belly. She appeared much older than someone in her mid-twenties and smelled like cigarettes and lavender-scented talcum powder.

My mother walked up to her without hesitating. "I want you to know that I will love this child as my own."

The woman nodded, almost in tears. "My husband died in a car crash right before I found out I was pregnant. This baby will be our second. I can barely take care of my first child. I wish it weren't this way, but it is."

"I promise I will honor your sacrifice my whole life."

It was that simple. Together, they went upstairs to the lawyer's office to make it all official. On the papers that they all had to sign, my mother found the word "sorrow" written in a box as explanation for the decision to give the baby up.

The baby's due date came and went. My mother began to worry that the woman had had second thoughts. At long last, the phone rang early on a Sunday morning in October 1961. The doctor said, "You got a healthy baby boy! But the mother, she's crying. You better send your husband quick or she might change her mind."

My father went with my mother's aunt Edna to name and claim the baby, because my mother, not formally identified as the mother, wasn't allowed by law to go. She trusted this aunt more than anyone else with the task of naming her child. The agreement was that the lawyer would then bring the baby to them. My parents did every-thing they were told, and two days later the lawyer appeared in their second-floor apartment with the newborn in his arms.

Peter was a big boy with a round, happy face and vivid blue eyes. Days, weeks, months passed, and still there was no final word on what they should do next to make the adoption fully legal. Their worry increased as the lawyer kept putting my parents off. And one day, they went to his office. My father asked my mother to wait in the car while he carried my brother inside.

"See this baby?" he said, holding Peter up so the lawyer could see him. "We want this baby to be ours in the law. He's already in our hearts."

"I understand."

"I don't think you do. Otherwise, you wouldn't be dragging your ass. Do you know how long we all wanted a baby?"

"I'll call you as soon as anything changes. Until then, I'm sorry, but you must wait."

So they did, but without legal authorization, they both felt increasingly afraid that someone would come and take Peter away. Their fear manifested itself like a bothersome ghost, causing my mother to lose sleep and my father to withdraw from her requests for physical affection, something he'd never done before. Still, they went forward with their lives. It helped that everyone in their family celebrated Peter's presence the way they would any new baby. Peter was going on six months before anyone noticed things that didn't seem right with him.

"He just lays there, Alice," my mother said to her best friend and cousin. "He doesn't roll, and his head is flat. I know some babies can have flat heads, but this is different. He doesn't move. He doesn't even seem to want to move."

"Such a love, huh?" Alice reached down to pick him up, and Peter giggled in delight.

No Meat Without the Bone

My mother pressed her face into his and Peter laughed a belly laugh, his cheeks turning red. "He is. But even if he tries, he can't roll. Alice, I'm getting worried."

"Have you taken him back to the doctor?"

"I did, but you know him. He just tells me everything's fine, it's first-time mother jitters. But I don't know . . ."

The combination of not being able to finalize the adoption with a growing concern for Peter's health began to bother everyone, but especially my mother. He still wasn't developing normally, and people in my parents' life started to say things. One night, after returning from a visit down South, Peter, then nine months old, ran a 105-degree temperature.

My mother was on the phone to the doctor instantly. "What should I do? He's burning alive!"

"Bring him to Children's Hospital immediately!" The doctor commanded her, and, in that moment, my mother grasped that he must have known something all along. Maybe he assumed Peter wouldn't live. Maybe he was worried that my parents would want their money back. Maybe he didn't do as good a job as the obstetrician who managed Peter's birth. They never found out.

They kept Peter at the hospital even after the fever subsided, to determine what was wrong with him. My mother stayed there with him for weeks, sleeping on a cot and calling home to report to my father. He never accompanied her on these visits to the hospital. He was drinking more. Maybe my mother was afraid of having him join her in a setting that could invite increased scrutiny. My father would lose his temper easily, and when things troubled him, he was more likely to come home drunk and mean.

She sat with Peter on her lap while the doctors finally gave her their assessment and recommendations. "Your son is severely, profoundly mentally retarded. He will be debilitated, and his condition will deteriorate dramatically over time. The sooner you can place him in an institution, the better. He won't live past three years of age."

My mother's heart raced, and her skin grew cold. "Is there something I can do? Some change in his diet? Some sort of physical therapy?" She knew it wasn't that simple, but the news was shattering.

Still, she decided to keep him. None of the doctors, with all their degrees and knowledge, supported her decision. They averted their eyes when speaking to her about all the medical needs my brother would have. Even so, she said, "I'm taking him with me, and we'll just see what happens." No one stopped her, and no one opened the door for her when she left. She felt sick to her stomach and knew she had to go home.

She climbed the stairs to their apartment slowly, touching each step with resolve the same way she prayed the rosary at night, feeling the wooden beads one at a time. Sometimes it really felt as if someone was listening. Was it Jesus, the son of Mary, or her own father, a tall man with kind eyes and large hands? Or was it her aunt the nun, feeling her struggle from thousands of miles away? Was she supposed to have become a nun as she had originally planned? Her life was unraveling in ways she had never dreamed. She wanted what was best for her family, but it was hard to know what to do.

She sat on the sofa with Peter on her lap and reached into the top drawer of the end table. She took out the Bible that her mom had given her when she received her confirmation. It was from Rome and bound in blood-red velvet. She laid the dense book across her belly, then placed Peter on top of it. He giggled and cooed as she looked up to the heavens through the low ceiling of her second-story apartment.

"If this is meant to be, Peter, then I am not going to give up on you." Then they both then fell fast asleep.

When she awoke, all her worry was gone.

No Meat Without the Bone

"From now until the end, we're in this with you, Peter." He smiled back at her, seemingly pleased with her decision.

The adoption proceedings continued to stall, and the fear my mother must have felt of being implicated in anything slightly prohibited, if not outright unlawful, made the struggles my dad posed seem insurmountable to her. Her heartfelt decision to keep and protect my brother further compromised her ability to challenge my dad, let alone seek help. This is when I imagine it began to matter less to my mother that my father was not the man she married, as long as she was, and always would be, Peter's mother. For my father, I understand today that his effort to earn a living, coupled with his longing to leave his past behind, drove his every move.

My parents didn't have a lot of money, nor did they have good insurance. In 1963, my mother brought Peter to the Franciscan Hospital for Children for the birth defects that were now becoming evident: cerebral palsy, scoliosis, muscular dystrophy, and mental retardation. Franciscan Hospital was a place that espoused the best possible outcome for children with special needs. Without a final adoption procedure, she still lived with the feeling that someone could simply come and take Peter away. They plugged along, hoping and praying that things would turn out all right. Days, weeks, months passed, and Peter kept living with a disarming level of sanguinity.

He underwent surgery on the muscles in his legs, a procedure that promised increased range of motion and limb control. My mother held his red and chapped hands while the anesthesia took effect. While he was operated on, she went grocery shopping with a good friend from nursing school to pass the time.

"I feel so nauseous," my mother said. "Maybe I didn't eat enough breakfast."

Her friend felt her forehead and checked her pulse. "No fever. Maybe it's just nerves."

Fortunate Daughter

But it wasn't. It was me. After giving up on the idea that she could conceive naturally, keeping Peter, and accepting the hardship of caring for him and the steady progression of my father's alcoholism, my mother gave birth to me in 1963. My sister Anna came along in 1964, and my youngest sister, Christina, in 1965. My mother became pregnant twice after that, but neither pregnancy carried to term. Finally, and without the church's permission, she had a full hysterectomy in 1970.

When I think of the people who became my parents, I realize they were many things that only now I am beginning to understand. I regard my mother's choice to stay married much the way I view how a seed chooses to become a tree: determined to live in the spot where it lands. Often it works. As for my father, remembering him, at times, is like standing on the shoreline of an unexpected tsunami. All I can see is the potential for destruction.

1968

Leftovers

1968, the year my first memories surfaced. My world was no bigger than the distance I could move without smelling my mother's coffee, or hearing my brother's laugh, or touching the top of one of my baby sisters' heads.

We lived in Somerville, in a two-family house owned by my parents on a street lined with two- and three-family homes. The Buccafuscos were our second cousins, and they lived upstairs from us. Mommy was best friends with Alice Buccafusco, her cousin-in-law through marriage. Vico, Alice's husband, was Mommy's real "blood cousin," Aunt Carmella's son.

I would often sneak up the back stairs after supper and knock softly on the door leading into the Buccafuscos' kitchen. I remember listening to the sound of Cousin Alice washing dishes. That's what all mommies did in the evening: wash dishes. Maybe their husbands were home, maybe they weren't. Maybe the wives knew where they were, maybe they didn't. Maybe it was nicer when their husbands weren't around. But mommies, mine and everyone else's, washed dishes.

"Oh, it's you," Cousin Alice said, acting surprised and drying her slender hands on a frayed cotton towel. "The boys are in the living room watching *Laugh In*."

I stood there, not knowing if she meant for me to come in or not. I didn't understand adults. They had a lot of rules about things. Sometimes it was okay to break those rules, sometimes not, and I wasn't a good judge as to when.

She touched my back, nudging me forward. "Go on, then; go on and see them."

Her three teenage sons, all of them beautiful, muscular, and black-haired, sat in a row on a dark-brown couch, staring at the black-and-white television. They turned their heads in unison as I entered the room. Each one had long lashes—"wasted on boys," Cousin Vico liked to say. He didn't like boys, especially the boys that were his sons. He wanted daughters. At the time, I thought that's why he treated my sisters and me so nicely. Maybe that's why he kissed me, right on the lips with his squishy, wet mouth. I didn't like it, but I didn't say so to anyone other than my sisters. I didn't say so to anyone about a lot of things.

I wore white polyester pajamas with a drawing of a cartoon elephant on the front. Water was squirting out of its trunk. Below the image was the phrase, "Sock it to me!" The oldest of the three boys, Vincenzo, reached out. "You want us to sock it to you, huh? Come over here!"

I ran over to him, afraid and thrilled at the same time. He grabbed me with strong hands and threw me across their laps. I loved how they smelled, a mixture of garlic, sweat, and after-shave. They took turns tickling me and pulling on my nose and toes as we sat and watched together.

Edith Ann, on the TV screen, sat in a huge rocking chair, pretending to write in an oversized diary. Her neighbors had banded together to get rid of the town's homeless. "Property values could plummet," they said. "A good neighborhood would be destroyed," they said. "Seems to me," said Edith Ann, "it would be a good neighborhood if we helped the homeless."

That's why I loved her; she understood how things should work and she said so. When I grew up, I wanted to be just like her, writing down my thoughts in a secret book with a fancy cover, revealing the truth about the world, the beautiful things I saw, the questions I had, and what I thought should be done about those people who would stop and gawp at my brother, Peter, every time we went anywhere.

Pio's breath smelled like cigarette smoke. He was the youngest and the one who got into the most trouble. My hair was standing straight up, filled with static from my pajamas, and my feet were sweaty. I loved those boys, partly because I knew they would never, ever really hurt me. They also lived in fear of their daddy. They didn't tell me this, but I could feel it, especially when Cousin Vico was around.

"Let her go now, boys," Cousin Alice said, pretending that she was really worried, even though I knew she wasn't. When she was worried, she crumpled paper tissues in her hands. "Go back downstairs, now. Your mommy is probably wondering where you are."

I shivered as I shuffled out of the living room into the kitchen. The refrigerator was open, and ice formed on the outside of the little freezer at the top. I had overheard my mother talking to Cousin Alice the day before. Cousin Vico gambled so much that they sometimes didn't have enough money to pay their bills or buy groceries. I didn't really understand what gambling was, outside of Pio pitching pennies against the back wall of the corner store with his buddies. Why could he gamble, and it was okay, but his daddy gamble and it was not?

I looked down from the top of the stairs. Cousin Alice yelled, "Rose, she's coming back." I often heard Marco, the middle son, come running down the stairs when his daddy wanted to beat him. Mommy would leave our door unlocked so he could come in and hide, at least until his daddy left to visit the local convenience store, where he met a man who made books. I thought this was strange because I'd never seen Cousin Vico read.

Fortunate Daughter

I took one step, not holding the banister the way Mommy taught me, and then I was flying, rolling, tumbling down the stairs. Nothing got in my way until I landed at the bottom. Though I felt dizzy, nothing hurt.

Mommy ran out of the kitchen where she was doing dishes, too, and knelt to pick me up. "You sure took the hard way down. Are you all right? Peter told me you had wandered upstairs. I was too busy with your little sister to go and get you." I pressed my face into her chest as she felt the back of my head for bumps.

"I'm okay, Mommy." I wanted to be hurt more badly so I could keep lying there like a little kitten getting licked by the mother cat.

"You've got an egg, little chicken. I'll get some ice." She stood up quickly; Anna was crying. Anna cried a lot, sometimes sounding like a kitten herself, but more often like the blender Mommy used to make us milkshakes. That's why Daddy brought home the rocking chair. To help Mommy help Anna not cry so much.

"How 'bout you go to bed now?" she said, when she came back with some ice cubes wrapped in a towel. "I still have to put Anna to sleep and Daddy still isn't home."

"Where is he, Mommy?" I often wondered, what did he do after he worked? I'd never met any of his friends. Did he have friends?

"Oh, never mind, Rose-Marie. Move along. Your brother's already asleep."

Back then, we walked to Mass at Immaculate Conception every Sunday as a family. The church was located just around the corner, and everyone in my neighborhood, all of whom were Catholic, walked as well—a Catholic parade, of sorts. I'd sit in the family pew and fold my hands in solemn prayer, head covered in a white veil that looked just like the dining-room tablecloth Mommy made, only smaller. The God I believed in was the Father, Son, Holy Ghost, Tooth Fairy, Santa Claus, and the Easter Bunny, all rolled into one.

Leftovers

There wasn't a thing I couldn't share with Him, including how bad I felt about ruining the sheets with a permanent red marker or how worried I'd become about a neighbor girls' interest in Anna.

As a little girl, I was dead set on growing up. I imagined that life would be much simpler. Adults had fewer commandments to follow, and even when they made mistakes, they were the ones running the show. Each night when I said my prayers before falling asleep, I would offer one Hail Mary for the naughty things I did.

During this time, Daddy, tall-legged and brawny, worked as a mill worker and truck driver. When he came home late from working second shift, Mommy would, most often, leave leftovers out for him, and I would stand in the shadow of the kitchen doorway and watch him eat. He washed down large bites of pasta in a red sauce with even bigger gulps of beer. He was done when he pushed the gold-flowered Corel plate away and looked for one of the heavy glass ashtrays that sat in every room of our house. I peered around the corner with rapt attention as he crossed his legs with the first inhale. It was only then that he would acknowledge my presence and motion for me to come over to him. While sitting on his lap during one of these moments, I was permitted my first taste of alcohol. Four years old and drinking with Daddy.

"You like how that tastes?" he asked, a smile on his face.

"I do, Daddy. It smells like you. It smells like bread."

"Made from the same stuff."

"Let her go to bed, Ned." Mommy said from the doorway, this time with Christina cradled in her arms. "She shouldn't be up at this hour." She looked tired so much of the time, like she could fall asleep standing up the way horses do. I didn't care. I wanted to stay with Daddy, and she was taking me away from him.

"Give me that." He took the Schlitz can from my hand. "Get yourself to bed." He got up and slapped Mommy's bottom gently. "I'll come along soon."

Fortunate Daughter

Papa Fabio, my grandfather, made his own wine in the basement of his home on Wallace Street. The scent of the oak barrels was enough to make me climb down there, despite my fear of the dark. I lay my head on the rough wooden lids and inhaled the cool, ripe smells. All family gatherings, christenings, first communions, and confirmations included large amounts of Papa Fabio's wine.

I didn't understand why Daddy's drinking had begun to make Mommy upset. He wasn't particularly unkind or harsh with us kids. If anything, drinking seemed to make him laugh and play with us more. Not just with his own children, but my cousins, too. He could often be seen down on the floor with more than one child on his back and another one hanging from his neck.

This one time, Daddy and Cousin Marco took down an oak tree in the side yard. They used a big, chattering, smoky chainsaw on a cool, wet day in the early spring. I felt sad when they started cutting off limbs.

"The tree has to go, Rose-Marie, it's sick," Daddy told me, but it didn't help. I liked trees so much, I wanted to grow up and be a tree. When I thought no one could see me, I wrapped my arms around the base of big trees and whispered prayers to the Almighty that I might become a tree if only for a moment, stretching my limbs into the heavens. I really liked this oak because I could stand below it and watch the branches sway and dance in the wind. The leaves looked like little clusters of stars.

The chainsaw stopped, and Daddy carefully climbed down holding something I couldn't see. I heard the "peep-peep" sound of baby birds before I saw them.

"A nest of blue jays," he said, holding them tenderly in his two big hands.

"Yea, we could've cut right through them," Marco said, his breath forming little clouds in the cold air.

Leftovers

The birds' mouths were open, eyes tightly closed, and their necks seemed too small to hold up their big heads. Their yellow-trimmed beaks looked like someone had painted them on.

"Why don't you bring these young'uns inside, Rose-Marie, otherwise they'll surely freeze to death." Daddy turned back to the tree with Marco.

I carried the nest inside, and Mommy took me in the pantry. She set the nest into a Maxwell House coffee can and put it on top of the washing machine. I lowered the can, so Anna and Christina could have a peek.

Anna said, "Der's twee a dem," and grabbed hold of Christina's hand and then mine. Just like my mom with her sisters, we three used to touch each other when we were feeling happy or sad or angry or anything.

"Mawida, Ana, and Tina-baby," Christina said, eyes open wide.

"Only I can move this can," I said, with a serious four-year-old, older-sister voice. I checked on the birds throughout the day, peering down at them in between brushing my hair and pretending to be Annette Funicello from *Beach Blanket Bingo*.

Then, that evening, I went into the pantry and couldn't find the can. "Where are the birdies, Mommy?"

She looked at Daddy as he sat at the table smoking a Pall Mall. He smiled and said, "I put them in another tree. Their mommy needed to find them. She wouldn't know where to look anywhere but in trees."

I ran from the room and threw myself on my bed, crying. I loved those birdies. I was going to raise them in this perfect world where no one would ever do anything to hurt them. I was going to keep them safe and warm. They were going to be mine and grow up and keep me company.

I heard Daddy come in behind me. "It's okay, Rose-Marie," he said softly. "They'll be happier growing up the ways birdies ought to. Why don't you read me a story? How 'bout this one here?" He held up *Go, Dog. Go!*

I had just learned how to read on my own, and this story was one of my favorites. He knew that, and with his arm around me, I went from feeling sad to proud. Daddy had a way of knowing just what to do to help me feel better.

Mr. Danger Man

I was five in 1969. That was when we packed all our furniture into a U-Haul hitch, crammed the rest of our stuff, including all six of us, into the station wagon, and moved to Morganton, a suburb in North Carolina, just south of where my father grew up and most of his family still lived.

Morganton was completely different from Somerville: cul-de-sacs with red-brick ranch houses and attached carports on streets without sidewalks and quiet nights. When Daddy would come home from working third shift at the Carbon Mills, Mommy would leave for work at a rehabilitation residence for young children whose parents had made the decision that they should live elsewhere, given the severity of their disabilities. Anna, Christina, Peter, and I did our best to keep a low profile while Daddy slept through the morning. We wandered in the woods across the street, playing house or hide-and-seek, or watched *Family Affair* with the volume low in the living room.

One morning, Christina and I were in the kitchen getting a snack. As we reached into the refrigerator, I spilled a whole container of Hawaiian Punch all over the linoleum floor. Christina covered her mouth—she hated messes more than anything. After we did our best to wipe it up, I decided we should use some Ajax to get rid of the stickiness. That's what Daddy would do. He liked using chemicals to clean his car, the casement windows in the basement, or the kitchen countertops. Often, Mommy would usher us outside at times, because she thought the smell would make us sick. So, Christina and I began furiously scrubbing that floor with Ajax and a wet sponge. It wasn't until we finished that we noticed the deep-red circular patterns in the shape of our arm motions. Daddy stood between the hall and the kitchen, quiet like a big empty house, chest bare and trousers wrinkled. His half-closed eyelids made it hard for me to know what mood he was in until he spoke. "What the hell are you young'uns up to?"

Christina and I didn't say a word. The quiet made me squirm. Daddy and Mommy had been fighting more lately. I'd listen when they thought we were all asleep. Sometimes Daddy could sound so fierce. But I was the oldest, and it had been my idea to clean the floor, so I thought I should answer him.

"I asked you something!" he yelled.

"Daddy, we had a —" and before I could finish telling him, he swung his right leg behind Christina and kicked her hard. She flew across the floor like a rag doll, landing against the breakfast island with a thud, then curled up and cried. I knelt, frozen like a statue. I had never seen him act so mean before. Neither of us moved. I watched Daddy walk toward the glass sliding doors that led out of the kitchen into the backyard, reaching into his front pocket for his cigarettes. He lit one up and turned his gaze out into the backyard.

I crawled over to where Christina lay and whispered, "Go in the bathroom. I'll clean up. Wash your face and I'll make something good. You want me to fix hamburgers? Mommy made some this morning and put them in the fridgerator. I'll let you slice the tomatoes to go on 'em." I shook, I was so frightened, and my voice trembled, too. But more so, I wanted to hurt Daddy. I felt something inside me start to vanish like early snow on black tar.

Anna, too, seemed to see things the way that I did, but instead of being more watchful, she went on the offensive. While Daddy grew more pugnacious, she got up in arms, and who could blame her? He would go out of his way to get her goat. Sometimes she would even yell back at him for bugging Mommy, something we understood as a dodgy prospect. When he was drunk, a time the rest of us knew to duck for cover, she'd become even more contemptuous, challenging him about everything.

Like the day she found a mole that had died in the backyard. She had dressed it up like a doll, pale-blue bonnet and everything, and she'd been cradling it in her arms like a baby.

"What the hell are you doing?" I heard Daddy ask her. "We've got to bury that thing, Anna; it's nothing but a dead animal." He said.

"No, Daddy, it's my baby," she said, drawing it closer to her chest.

I'd been standing by the back door, eating an apple and watching. I could see what was coming and knew not to interfere. He went into the house and came back with a belt, not the one he wore around his waist.

"I said put that thing down, so we can get rid of it properly." The belt hung by his side.

Her bottom lip quivered but she held her ground. "I can bury my baby."

Daddy grabbed her by the shoulders. The animal, tiny and small, flew out of her arms like it had wings, and I thought that it had magically turned into a bat. She reached out for it just as Daddy struck her hard on the back of her legs. She screamed, and he yelled at her to be quiet. That's when she charged him, but he was ready for her, the corners of his mouth lifted in a smile like he was finally getting the reaction he wanted. I sprinted toward her from the house, screaming, "Run, Anna, run away! Daddy is no one! Daddy is no one!" even though I knew that wasn't true. He was the opposite of no one in our lives. He was everyone and everywhere.

Fortunate Daughter

Mommy finally heard the commotion from inside the house and came running out. She was helping Peter into his leg braces.

"What are you doing?" she yelled at Daddy.

I wanted to say, "What he always does, Mommy," but I lacked Anna's courage for speaking my mind. Besides, it was hard to tell what was going to happen, sometimes. Just when I thought I'd figured out a way to determine the course of things, something else happened that proved me wrong. Daddy lost his grasp on the belt, and Anna scooped up the mole from where it had fallen. She pressed it against her chest and the paws opened as if to comfort her. She was crying still, and I felt confused. I didn't know it then, but I yearned for safety. The safety that Mommy was unable to provide, again and again. The safety I imagined other children, mostly the ones I saw on TV, had and took for granted. The safety that Daddy had no intention of giving his children. He was Mr. Danger Man with a capital D, which was why I felt unsafe, even in my own skin, especially in my own skin. Peeled bare like an apple. Daddy could appear at any time. Sometimes, it was a good thing. But more often, it was coming to mean something bad. I didn't understand why: It was just how it was.

1969

Love Might Have Nothing to Do with It

Anna and I were close, but we did not always enjoy one another's company. Many times, I resented her for not accepting her place as younger than me, less aware, less mature. This one time, when we still lived in Somerville, we raced one another, me on my bicycle and her running beside me trying to keep up. Somehow, she moved in front of me, thinking she could block my way. When she tripped, I rode right over her, pressing her face flat like a grilled-cheese sandwich. I knew it was a naughty thing to do, but I was glad to win the race and, more importantly, teach her a lesson that would warrant repeating over the years. *I am older than you, little sister; you shall not prevail*, I remember thinking to myself.

I remember the yard behind our red-brick ranch, larger in my mind's eye than I'm certain it was. I'm kneeling in the dirt with her, visiting all manner of terror on ant lions we'd discovered there, our breath raising havoc with their neatly funneled sand homes. Inhaling the earthy smell of Anna's curly brown hair and watching her normally round cheeks expand like balloons is what I carry still. That afternoon, we were a team as we chanted in unison:

Fortunate Daughter

Doodlebug, doodlebug
Run away home!
Your house is on fire
our children alone.

Those rhymes we learn as youngsters resonate in ways that we don't understand at the time. Mommy came out on the back stoop, took a deep breath of the thick summer air, and let it out. "Who wants ice cream?" Her long black hair, tied in a bun, frizzed around her face because the humidity. She'd let me brush it out for her that morning. Anytime I could make her feel good, it tickled me.

Anna and I jumped up and ran ahead of her to the carport. I was standing with Mommy, trying not to scratch the chigger bites behind my bony knees when Daddy's truck pulled into the driveway.

I knew he was drunk by the way he stared at us through the windshield, like he was looking through us. Mommy's body stiffened as if she was suddenly playing freeze tag.

Daddy's door swung open slowly, and his heavy work boots covered in thick red clay landed on the driveway. A gray metal lunchbox hung like a big, ugly charm-bracelet charm from his black leather belt.

"Where y'all off to in such a hurry?" he asked, lifting his face upward. A light mist fell from the sky, and warm, moist air circled around us. A storm was coming.

"We're going to get ice cream. It's humid and the kids have been asking all week," Mommy said calmly. "Your supper's on the stove. I made grilled hamburgers and beans just the way you like 'em."

Anna, Christina, Peter, and I got the message and did our best to scramble into the '65 Ford Country Squire station wagon, pretending we were just going out for dessert, not running and hiding. Peter, though older than me by three years, moved his crutches and leg braces slowly.

Love Might Have Nothing to Do with It

Funny thing was, before Daddy arrived, Mommy had tried to delay our supper, I guess so that he could join us. At least, that's what I thought Mommy wanted. Otherwise, why would she have stalled the way she did? It was getting harder and harder to figure her out. Most of the time, I liked it better when he didn't join us. We laughed more, and Mommy didn't scold us as much, even when I got Christina to laugh so hard that Kool-Aid ran out of her nose. It was almost seven-thirty by the time we finished eating, and Daddy still wasn't home. Mommy washed the dishes and went in the bedroom to put on her wig, the style at that time, while we raced to clear the table and then went out to play. Nothing like the promise of going out to move us along, and I knew it would be easier all around if we were gone before Daddy got home.

I was right. He said, "I'm going with y'all," and took a big swig out of a fluorescent orange soda can and crushed it in one hand. There was no discussion as he slid onto the front passenger's seat. I got in the back seat with Peter. Anna and Christina sat in the rear, facing the tailgate, Christina's braids lying against her small shoulders like the twine I used to learn cat's cradle. My sisters liked to sit together and look out the back window and wave at cars. Mommy turned to back out of the driveway, her sheet-white knuckles gripping the seat back behind Daddy's head.

We weren't in the car more than a few minutes when he said, "I keep telling you to use your rearview mirror. When are you ever going to listen to me?" Then he reached over and poked his thick finger into her cheek like he was testing to see if she was ripe. I couldn't stand what a bully he was in these moments. It also made me feel like a traitor to enjoy his company when he was being nice. How could I love someone, love being with him, and doing things that he liked or, better still, that I liked, who earlier—sometimes that same day—had made our lives hellish? It took me many years to learn how not to feel responsible for loving him, loving both my parents, despite the ways they hurt me and my siblings.

Thunder rumbled as we drove down streets with no sidewalks. I wondered what my father dreamt, his eyes now closed and his breath deepening. Was he chasing a bear with dogs and a gun? He'd tell my siblings and me stories about long and involved hunting trips with his daddy, my grampa. I'd often then dream about a bear chasing me through dark woods. Sometimes my daddy would shoot him before he got me, but sometimes I'd wake up in a cold sweat, being swallowed whole.

Rain poured out of the sky, and the water that trickled down the windows appeared to move on my arm. I pretended my whole body could become liquid and drip. My legs stuck to the tan vinyl seat and I lifted them slowly, watching my skin stretch like thin dough.

"Will da rain let up when we get dere?" Christina asked in her baby voice.

I rolled my eyes. "Only God knows things like that."

Daddy, now awake, kept reaching over and jabbing at Mommy. He acted sort of playful, but I could tell it hurt her. Maybe he was bored or just being plain mean. In a funny sort of way, I understood him. I, too, sometimes enjoyed hurting the ones I loved. But understanding him didn't make me feel any better. I looked away, as if by not looking at what Daddy was doing, I could make it disappear like magic. Watch me pull a rabbit out of my hat!

I had the constant example of Mommy, also acting as if he wasn't doing anything. She was good at that, especially when Daddy was the one to blame. Maybe it was her way of trying to make it easier on all of us.

"Why don't you sing 'Old MacDonald Had a Farm'?" she asked Peter.

He immediately complied in a high-pitched voice, playing

along with the game of acting normal, or knowing that he wasn't; to this day, I don't know which it was.

"Old MacDonald had a farm, ee—ii—ee—ii—oo . . . and on that farm he had a cow . . . with a moo, moo here . . . and a moo, moo there . . . "

He was still singing when we pulled into the local ice cream shop. A bunch of cars with steamy windows idled in the parking lot, each one filled with families waiting for the storm to let up.

With eyes still closed and arms folded across his chest, Daddy said, "Go on. Get the kids some ice cream. That's what you came here for!" When his voice rose, we took our cue to become silent.

Suddenly, I imagined the boneyard near Gramma's house. Daddy brought me there, so I could learn the names of people in our family who had passed long ago. The quiet in that cemetery, like the quiet in the car, frightened me, but Daddy had his reasons for bringing me there. Reasons I didn't understand.

"I thought I'd wait for the storm to pass," Mommy murmured and looked at him sideways. I couldn't stand her, even though I knew hating anyone, let alone Mommy, was a sin. Why didn't she stand up for herself? Why didn't she tell him to take a long walk on a short pier? Why didn't she assume her rightful place?

"Well, you thought wrong." He threw a ten-dollar bill at her, and it fluttered to the floor. When she bent down to pick it up, he grabbed her by the back of her neck and held her there. She screamed, and he laughed, giving her neck a little shake.

I leaned over the front seat, closer to Daddy's beer-sweat. "Give me the money," I said. "I'll get the ice cream."

His grasp slackened, and he looked right at me. I stared into his russet brown eyes. It was like considering my own, but his were dark in anger. I shivered, but I kept my gaze. It made me tremble. I could get slapped full in the face, but I didn't care. I couldn't stand how he tormented us. He wasn't so tough or brave, not like my kindergarten classmate, Rudolph, with his shiny black skin, who stayed at his desk when the scary witch came on Halloween and sent the rest of us, teacher included, screaming to the far corner of the room. Or like Anna, convincing me to learn the song "Yankee Doodle Dandy" so that we might perform at our preschool graduation. She made some of the words naughty and sang them loudly as we stood beside one another. Our teachers chuckled, but Daddy got mad at us. She agreed to go first for a switching, because it was her idea in the first place. No, Daddy wasn't so tough.

He handed me the money but wouldn't let go of my hand. I imagined spitting on him, even though I knew that wouldn't be good manners. So I just held my breath and counted silently, waiting to see what would happen. One, two, three . . .

Seconds later he let me go, and I jumped out of the car. Just then, lightning flashed over my head, so bright it seemed someone had taken a picture. Maybe it was God keeping track of things with a big camera in the sky. If the angels could bowl, I was sure God could log our small lives in any one of many ways. Then the crash of thunder, deafening.

I ran to the store window, and the fat woman standing inside said, "Lord have mercy, child, why'd your pappy send you over here now? The ice cream'll still be cold in five more minutes." She looked at me, waiting for me to say something. When I didn't, she handed me a soft, white cloth and said, "What can I get you, darling?" We'd moved from Somerville to North Carolina, and the sound of her voice, rich with a southern drawl, was soothing even still.

I wiped my face and clutched the wet rag. I gave Daddy's order first, to guarantee that his would melt first. Butter pecan in a cup. Anna liked chocolate in a cone, no sprinkles. Christina liked vanilla with sprinkles. Peter wanted strawberry in a cup. I liked maple walnut with sprinkles, too. What did Mommy want? How come I

Love Might Have Nothing to Do with It

couldn't remember? I panicked for a moment and then decided on coffee, remembering she drank coffee in the morning.

The woman handed me everything in a cardboard box. The rain had slacked off, and the sound of thunder was farther away. My sneakers made wet, mushy sounds on the way back to the car. Mommy reached back to open the door for me, and I got in quickly. Christina and Anna both wanted theirs right away, but I made them wait, just for sounding impatient. As I handed Daddy his ice cream, he asked, "Where's the change?" and I gave it to him without speaking. I was busy trying to figure out what had happened while I was gone, because I knew how things could go from bad to worse quickly when Daddy was drunk. Then I saw the mark of his hand on the right side of Mommy's face.

She left her ice cream in the box and, sniffling, put the car in reverse. The rain started again.

"The storm is coming back around," Daddy said, sounding pleased.

I licked my ice cream without really tasting it and put a hand on Mommy's left shoulder, perched like a mourning dove on a telephone wire. I wanted to take care of her, stroke her forehead, and bring her room-temperature ginger ale and a soft blanket, like she did for us kids when we'd be feeling sick or tired. I wanted her life, my life, just this hour to be so much better than what it was. The longing for a different life became a pastime for many years.

A few minutes passed before I realized we were going home a different way.

"Why are we going on this road?" I asked.

"Your daddy wants us to go this way, Rose-Marie. Please just be quiet," she said, with irritation in her voice. I felt snubbed and betrayed.

We must have been on a hillside as the road twisted and turned. Mommy's voice rose. "I don't think I can do this. Let me pull over. I'll let you drive."

"Dammit, you're the one who wanted to get ice cream. Don't start your bitching with me!" He jerked the steering wheel hard.

Everything happened in slow motion. The car rolled once, twice, three times, maybe more. My head was on the ceiling and then it wasn't. Glass shattered, and metal bent. Screams flew like sparks. Then I was lying on the ceiling. My left shoulder ached, and I couldn't move it. Rain pitter-pattered on the bottom of the car when Daddy started kicking his door open.

"Get us out of here," Mommy whispered. Her head was next to mine and her breath felt hot on my face. Peter was quiet, but my sisters yelled, "Get us out, too, Daddy! Get us out, too!"

I was starting to be able to make sense of things. The car lay upside down in a patch of sweet-smelling woodbine, wild roses, and poison ivy. Something else smelled, too. It made my nose burn and my eyes water. Blood dripped down on Daddy's face, in his eyes and on his nose and lips. He reached into the car like a bear searching frantically for honey and attempted to retrieve my sisters and brother. I felt scared, but there was no way I was going to leave Mommy.

"Go up to the road, girls, and wave someone down," he ordered.

"What about Mommy?" Christina asked. "Get Mommy too?"

"I'll get her. Just do what I tell you," Daddy said, louder this time.

I used my right arm and pulled myself over to the door where my siblings got out. Daddy reached his arm down to help me, but I jerked my hand away. I wanted his help least of all. He was the reason we were in this mess.

"Help Mommy," I said, clear as ice.

He reached past me and pulled her by the legs. Her knees bled, and her skirt scrunched up around her waist. The wig she'd put on before going out had fallen off, revealing black hair, neatly tied in a bun.

Daddy stooped down now so Peter could pull himself up onto

his back, and then trudged up the embankment. I took Mommy's hand and we began to climb. The headlights of a car moved in a slow arc at the top of the hill and then stopped. Anna and Christina must have waved someone down. My heart was pounding from the slippery climb when I saw a red pickup truck.

"I'll call the police and get an ambulance," said an elderly man with hair white as marshmallows. "Ya'll look pretty beat up."

"No," Daddy said, his tone softer, charming even. "We'll manage just fine if you wouldn't mind giving us a lift home."

The man stared back at him for what seemed like forever. Then he rubbed his chin with a wrinkled and freckled hand. I wondered how he got so many freckles without having any on his face. I imagined his house as bigger than ours, like the one from *Bonanza,* and just like Ben Cartwright, he lived on a million-acre ranch with a bunch of dogs, and horses in the pasture that children could ride bareback whenever they wanted.

"I can respect your wishes to a certain point," he said. "But I want to get your young'uns to a hospital before you go anywhere else tonight." He sounded certain. I wanted him to take me home. I wished he were my daddy.

Daddy sighed and helped all us kids into the front seat of the man's truck. He took Mommy to the rear of the truck and climbed in after her. The rain cleared up and stars began to dot the evening sky. Christina cried softly, and Anna grasped her hand. A sharp pain in my left shoulder made me wince every time the truck turned a corner, but I felt relief in knowing that the accident was behind us. I wondered where my ice cream sat, thinking wherever it was, it had remained sweet and unharmed. Peter, in his dull understanding of the world, seemed unfazed by the ordeal and asked the man, "Can we watch doctor fix Mommy and Daddy's boo-boos?"

"Can't rightly tell, son; hospitals are places with rules you can't always predict. You young'uns were lucky tonight. Lucky as a dime."

■·—·—·■

We all piled out at the emergency entrance of the hospital and slowly made our way through the glass doors. Daddy's face was lined with dried blood, which flaked like old paint. When examined by the nurse attendant in the hallway, he shrugged and said, "Aw, it's just superficial."

When they called my name, both Daddy and Mommy rose and followed me into the examination room. The doctor explained that my shoulder had dislocated.

"I can set it pretty easily, but you both may want to step outside," he said, and every muscle in my body stiffened. It was going to be bad! I knew it! It's never good when they ask your parents to leave.

"I'd just as soon stay," Daddy said, and Mommy stroked my cheek before going back out into the waiting room, as if that was enough, as if my brother and sisters needed her more than I did. Daddy moved close enough that I could feel the weight of his body leaning up against the shoulder that wasn't injured, and I propped myself up as best I could. The popping sound was loud, and when my shoulder joint snapped back where it belonged, I held my breath and nearly fainted. I couldn't help thinking how much I would have preferred being at home, watching *Chitty Chitty Bang Bang*, my hands still sticky from ice cream that had dripped onto my fingers.

When we came back out into the waiting room, Anna asked Mommy, "What's 'supersisal'?"

"Superficial, honey. It means skin deep."

I asked, "Is that the same thing as superstitious?" I loved words then, all words—how you could say one thing and mean another or think something and not say it or use a different word and not get into trouble. Words gave meaning, even amid a calamity, especially when things were upside-down. I wanted always to know

definitions, and I listened to what Mommy told Anna with attention that I hoped no one would detect.

"No," she said, "that's something else entirely. That means
believing in something that's not real."

"Like a car crash, Mommy?" Christina asked.

"Where we all could have died," Anna chimed in, and we sat
down.

"What's it called when you *almost* die?" I asked, trying not to
look Anna in the eye for fear that she'd see my anger.

"Lucky," Mommy said, "Lucky you're alive."

I didn't feel lucky. I felt mad and hungry and my shoulder
ached. Just because Mommy wanted to look on the bright side of
this "luck dime" didn't mean I would. I refused to be cheerful.

1970

Broken Crayons

Not long after the car accident, Mommy's father, Papa, was diagnosed with Alzheimer's. His decline, heartbreaking and devastating, along with Mommy's growing fear about Daddy's drinking, meant we packed up and moved back to Somerville, the place where Mommy was born and raised, where she thought she'd be more comfortable, more understood, safer even.

Though raised Catholic, I'd never attended Catholic school and had no idea what was in store for me. I was six years old, entering the first grade late.

"Welcome, Rose-Marie, to our classroom," Sister Catherine said in a quiet voice, looking down at me on my first day. Not that she had far to look. She was tiny and covered from head to toe in thick black robes tied at the waist with what looked like rope. Her black habit framed her face such that she seemed to be peering out from behind curtains on a stage. I wondered for many years what the bodies of these nuns really looked like and how much time it took them to get dressed in the morning. I imagined that she must be sweaty, and I nervously extended my hand, which she placed in her own. Her thin bones felt like dead twigs that fell from trees in a windstorm. And her veins were thick like spaghetti that Mommy's mother, Nana, made.

"Little people, attention!" she called.

Broken Crayons

It looked to me like the children were already paying attention, but they folded their hands and brought their knees together in one motion—a custom I, too, would develop in response to the voice of my teacher.

"This is Rose-Marie. She is going to join us for the rest of this school year. I expect that every one of you will do your best to make her feel a part of our classroom. Receive her as Christ receives you, a member of the community of the Lord to which we all belong, for she, too, is a child of God." Her words had a singsong quality to them, as if they'd been spoken many times before.

For almost a year, my family and I lived in Nana and Papa's house on Wallace Street. Every house on that street was filled with large Irish- or Italian-Catholic families. Papa died that spring, the year prisoners at Attica took hostages, Mt. Etna erupted, and Disney World opened in Florida. The purple and white lilacs were in full bloom, and their fragrance lingered in the warm, wet air that blew in my bedroom window. I sat in the living room on Nana's scratchy horsehair couch, listening and watching grown men and women tearfully tell stories of how Papa had helped them over the years.

At the funeral, Nana threw herself in the casket where Papa lay looking like a statue; and in the weeks that followed his death, I'd brace myself for the cheek-pinching that ensued when my great-aunts and -uncles from the "old country" paid their respects. I liked their attention, but it was rare that their touch didn't leave a red mark.

"Where are you going?" Anna asked me as I attempted to sneak into the basement one afternoon when we were supposed to be outside.

"None of your business. Go back outside with Christina and Peter," I said, trying to sound commanding, but Anna was always one to spot trickery.

"I'll tell Mommy. You're not supposed to go down there without Papa . . . " She stopped. We both realized the criterion had changed.

Fortunate Daughter

I didn't really want to do anything; I just wanted to breathe in the odor of a damp basement floor and look at small Ball jars filled with even tinier screws and touch wine barrels that smelled musty and grapey. I wanted to be someplace safe, and that was Nana and Papa's basement, where I thought Papa still was. Often, when he was busy fixing a broken appliance or window sash, I would sneak up behind him. He wouldn't stop what he was doing, but I knew that he knew I was standing behind him. He would let me stand there for a few minutes, and then ask me to hand him a screwdriver or a hammer. "*Passami che.*" Papa never raised his voice, and he never said a bad thing about anyone.

With Papa, there had been no ambiguity about right or wrong or what it meant to truly care for a person. I was seeking out, if only in the scent of things that belonged to him, that clarity. Papa never tried to persuade me to believe that used crayons were as good as brand-new ones, or that that was all that I was worth. He was an honorable man who believed in the truth and kindness and consistently treated me as the child I was. With Papa, there was no fear of what I'd lose or must compromise.

There was only the feel of his beard against my face when he kissed me goodnight, which, come morning, I would still sense.

There was the touch of his strong hands, as he played thumb wars with my cousins and me, allowing us merely to come close to winning.

There was the smell of wine and garlic on his breath, even when he hadn't recently drunk or eaten either.

There was the delight in knowing that he loved all his grandchildren, and he only loved me.

There was the sound of his laugh when he thought an idea was asinine, especially a political thought or the insensitive remark of a foolish guest.

Broken Crayons

There was the rhythm of his walking when he left the living room to retire for the night.

There was the wonder of his private life with Nana and his ability to ground her in feeling grateful and kind.

There was the vague sense that his leaving would mean a broken heart for my mother, one she never really recuperated from.

There was the teasing, gentle and consistent on his part, toward all those who tried to make things unnecessarily subdued.

There was the echo of the Italian Diaspora in his whole being that resulted in his family fleeing Naples at the turn of the twentieth century.

There was a yearning for him to be more than my grandfather, a yearning for him to be my father.

1971

Faster Than You

"Tell us a story, Daddy," Christina shouted. Daddy was helping Peter get undressed, and my sisters and I came into his room to say goodnight, a nightly ritual of sorts. Mommy was in the hospital and sick, like Papa was right before he died. I hoped she wouldn't die, too. She was rushed off to the hospital by one of my uncles in the middle of the night, burning with fever.

"All right, it'll have to be a quick one," Daddy said and sat on the end of Peter's bed, still wearing his work clothes. Anna, Christina, and I sat on the floor.

"I must have been about your age," he said pointing to Peter, "and I'd been in the woods awhile. I had my gun, but I didn't have my dog. I heard some rustling off in a patch of blackberries. I walked real soft and peered through some tall grass."

"What you see?" Peter asked.

"Just you wait." He paused, stretching it out. "There were two black bear cubs having a time trying to get some ripe berries off those bushes. They were probably only forty pounds or so, and real cute. I sat there thinking there's nothing better than this, when I heard a growl."

"From where, Daddy?" Christina asked, scrunching up close to me.

"Too close, and right behind me."

"What did you do?" I asked.

"I took off out of there like an underfed mountain cat chasing supper."

"Did you get away?" Christina asked, leaning forward now.

"Of course, he did," I said. "He wouldn't be here telling us this story if he hadn't."

"Very good, Rose-Marie. But I didn't do it by running. A black bear worried about her cubs will always run faster than you."

"What did you do?" we asked in unison.

"I ran up a tree, which is what you all should do right now before I make supper out of you!" He then ran after us, pretending he was going to eat us.

I missed Mommy, but Nana missed her more. She would sit at the kitchen table and cry and moan into daybreak, with both her other daughters doing their best to console her.

"They'll give her the care she needs, Ma," Auntie Gina said, stroking Nana's head.

"My Rosaria, my Rosaria," she kept repeating, as she leaned back with her eyes closed against Auntie Ada's chest.

I stood at the kitchen counter, piling toasted Italian bread on a plate, going heavy on the butter and sugar that Mommy would only let us have on special occasions. Mommy being in the hospital seemed pretty special to me. But then days passed, and it stopped feeling special.

My sisters and brother and I finished lunch one day, and I helped Nana kill and clean the eels for supper that night and then followed her into the pantry. She wasn't crying as much, but she still acted like she wanted someone with her all the time. She'd lost Papa, her one true love, and now her oldest daughter was critically ill. I was headed to the basement, the place where Papa used to sharpen knives on a coarse stone wheel. I loved watching the sparks fly off like fireworks.

Fortunate Daughter

"Help your brother get his braces on," Daddy yelled from the kitchen table.

"Where we going?" I asked him, trying to sound casual.

"To see your momma."

My heart leaped. It had been well over a week since we'd seen Mommy. None of us knew when or if Mommy was coming home. It turned out she was very ill with bacterial spinal meningitis. Anna and I didn't really know what that was, but we knew what it meant; she might not come home.

"We can't, Daddy; they don't let kids in the hospital, remember?" I didn't want what I was saying to be true, but I didn't want to be disappointed, either. Maybe he'd forgotten.

"You children need to see your momma. Just do as I say."

He was right. I missed Mommy more than anything, and I ran into my sister's room where I knew Anna and Christina were playing with their dolls.

"Get dressed. We're going to see Mommy. Daddy said so. I gotta get Peter ready!"

I grabbed Peter's braces and crutches from the corner of the parlor where he sat watching cartoons.

"Come on, Peter. Let's get ready." I began helping him take off his pajamas and then played "How many fingers do I have up?" while he did his best to extend his legs and reach his arms up over his head.

"You beautiful, Rose-Marie," Peter said. He said these sorts of things a lot. And he meant it, too. Normally, I didn't mind, but I wanted to leave lickety-split!

"You got to help me put these on, Peter. We're going to see Mommy."

"You like when I hug you." He had reached both his arms around my torso and was squeezing me tightly.

"I do, Peter, but you're squeezing me too tight." I started to wriggle to free myself. "Here, put your foot in this shoe, and I'll start your other leg. Help me, silly head. And remember, Mommy is sick."

When we got outside, the blue irises, awash with light, stood at attention, watching all of us children like sentries from the front of Nana's garden. Many of the neighbor kids were out playing on the street that day. A bunch of them, friends of ours, came running over to the driveway and stood with us below the catalpa trees in Nana and Papa's yard. We would often take turns pretending the long bean pods that dangled from our mouths were cigars, like the ones we'd seen our uncles smoke after eating Sunday dinner with the family.

"Want to play Relievio?" Tommy yelled.

"How 'bout Dodge Ball?" Connie asked.

"We have to go visit our mommy," I told them, before Anna and Christina could get their feet off the front steps leading onto the sidewalk. I had this awareness, deeply instilled, of being able to take control of a situation by being the first one to impart information. "Our mommy is very sick, and our daddy is taking us to visit her, so we can cheer her up."

Eddie said, "Aw, now we won't have enough players for prison camp."

"Shut up, Eddie; you are such a moron," Judy said. She was my age and the oldest of five. Then, looking above me, she asked, "Can we come, too?" A silent hush fell over everyone. I hadn't realized my daddy was standing near.

Without missing a beat, he said yes. I didn't know why. Maybe it was the part of him that would bring Mommy a new dog from the animal shelter across the street from the hospital every time she gave birth to a new baby. "Whoever wants to come, better get in the car right now."

The four of us, plus another half dozen kids, climbed into the back of the Chrysler Imperial station wagon. No one had to check with their parents, and we didn't have to wear seatbelts. We just piled in, one on top of the other, like a stack of newspapers. I had two kids sitting on top of me, and my belly felt so squished I thought I might puke, but I didn't say anything. We were going to see Mommy.

When we arrived at the hospital, Daddy parked on the street and told everyone to wait. He wasn't gone that long, but I felt sticky and my head hurt. When he came back, he opened the door and said, "All you young'uns get out of the car and stand here." He pointed to a chain-link fence that bordered the hospital.

"Is Mommy coming home, Daddy?" Christina asked. "Can she come home with us today?"

"Not today, but she'll get to see you and you'll get to see her."

I looked up at the window Daddy kept glancing toward. It was on the third floor, and one of the curtains was pulled back. That's when we saw her. Mommy, standing there wearing a thin cotton johnny, looking down at us wearing a smile, the biggest I'd ever seen. She waved and we all jumped up and down, waving back at her, blowing kisses, holding hands. I started to cry, but wiped my tears away quickly so no one could see.

I wondered how she felt, standing there at the window, the sun on her face, her cheeks red with fever, looking down at everyone, her children, other mommies' children. Right then and there, I felt a part of me not want to be there. All of us being there meant Mommy wasn't home. I felt a twinge of embarrassment and shame, and for the second time that day, I thought I might throw up. It didn't matter to me at all that Mommy didn't do a good job all the time; I just wanted her back.

"Mommy, Mommy!" Anna yelled first, and then all the children started waving. I pretended she was a queen staring out her castle window. Her smile, bright as day, and her hair all mussed up. She blew exaggerated kisses toward us, and Christina said, "I got it, Mommy. That one is mine."

Faster Than You

A clamp tightened around my heart. It didn't matter that we couldn't go inside. Peter and Christina didn't know that she might die, but Anna and I did. She had a serious illness, one that might take her away from us. I felt that if I lost her, then I might die, too. It didn't matter that Daddy and Nana were taking care of us. It didn't matter that we all felt closer. I wanted Mommy to come home and be my mommy again. I even told God that I would forgive her for not always keeping us safe. If she became well, fully well, then I'd give her another chance.

That night, I knelt on the floor beside my bed and prayed.

Please God don't let Mommy leave us. We need her to be our mommy. She cannot be our mommy if she's not here. Things will get a whole lot worse if she doesn't come home. A whole lot worse. Trust me, God. I know what I am talking about. You don't live here. You don't know. She takes care of us when we're sick. She makes us soup with big chunks of chicken and macaroni. She taught me how to tie my shoes the easiest way. And she can blow a bubble without popping it. Nobody else I know knows how to do that stuff. Please don't take our mommy.

Mommy finally returned home, but she looked a whole lot smaller than when she left. A crowd of neighbors clapped and cheered when she got out of the car, and Daddy gave her a bouquet of white carnations in front of everyone. After she kissed me good night that first evening, I lay in the stillness of my attic room and wondered about many things. Was Mommy's spirit weaker? If so, what was going to happen to us?

I wanted her to make things better in a lasting way. I wanted Daddy to keep acting the way he was when Mommy was in the hospital, so I wouldn't have to worry. I wanted Peter to be able to play in the street with me like all the other kids. I wanted the catalpa tree in Nana and Papa's backyard, branches shimmering with white blossoms, to bloom all year-round. But it wouldn't, and I knew it. Winter would come.

Mommy recovered from meningitis, and my parents began to search in earnest for a home of their own. They soon bought a two-family that needed a lot of work, down the street from Nana. We kept living with Nana while Daddy spent most of his free time at the house, patching, scraping, and painting. Mommy didn't like him being over there so much, I wasn't sure why. Maybe it was because she didn't like living with Nana. But he insisted it was easier to get it all done before we moved in. And, of course, he won.

He was also still drinking, which meant going anywhere with him could be treacherous. But that didn't stop me from wanting to be with him. When he offered to take me somewhere, I jumped at the opportunity. I was seven years old, and even though the chance of him behaving tenderly toward me was slim, I'd risk it. The other truth was rooted in my understanding that when Mommy wasn't around, he was more likely to be gentle and kind.

"Hand me one of them small scrapers." he said, staring down at me from near the top of a big aluminum ladder, right leg raised and bent, wearing a navy-blue one-piece. A cigarette dangled out of the corner of his mouth like a pointy hook latch. The air was cold, and my nose was running like a faucet. I was glad to be wearing warm, chocolate-brown wool gloves. They were my favorite and they smelled a little like paint. I liked that smell.

"Is this one okay?" I held up a paint scraper that fit nicely into my own hand.

"Yeah," he said. "Bring it on up here."

Though I felt a bit afraid to get on the ladder, it thrilled me to be able to give Daddy what he asked for. It was like we were in a perpetual contest. Would I be the daughter he wanted? Would he be the Daddy I needed? Climbing the ladder was a small price to pay to win this round.

Faster Than You

We spent the better part of the morning taking off the old, peeling paint on one side of the house and putting on a primer coat. I had no idea that spending a mid-November day house painting was unusual for a child my age or that the paint might not attach correctly due to the temperature. Work was what we did on the weekend.

I was hungry way before Daddy suggested we take a break, but I didn't say a word. Another item in my "good daughter" column.

"Reach into my pocket and I bet you'll find two Paydays," he said, pointing to a light-brown corduroy jacket swung over the first-floor porch banister. Daddy loved this candy bar. And because he loved it, so did I. It had a chewy, sweet center covered with salty peanuts. I handed him his and peeled the wrapper off mine. I don't have any photographs of what Daddy looked like when he ate this candy bar, but I wish I did. His expression, chewing and swallowing the sweet and salty nougat, will forever remain the definition of satisfaction.

He had a bottle of milk wedged between his feet, popped open the lid with no trouble, and took one swig. He looked at me out of the corner of his eye and said, "You wanting something to drink too?"

"Yep, I do," I said with a smile.

"Go on and get the other bottle in the car. I left it there for you."

I knew why Daddy wouldn't share his. A year earlier, I pestered him to give me a drink of his Coke until he finally relented. That was when I found out it was spiked with vodka. That was when I decided going thirsty was easier.

When I came back, Daddy was out behind the house. He had opened the two large bulkhead doors leading down into the basement.

I gaped into the darkness. "It looks kind of like a grave, Daddy."

He didn't speak, and instead walked down the steep stairs. I assumed that it was my cue to follow him. We descended, and I heard him mumble, almost to himself, that he needed to find some good paintbrushes.

The passageway that led into one of the storage areas was damp like Nana and Papa's basement. The walls were made of slate stone and mortar, with a dirt floor with boards running across it. I smelled the mold that grew in the recesses of these dark places, and I crinkled my nose.

Daddy said, "Why don't you put on some warmer clothes?"

I stopped dead. "I don't need different clothes, Daddy. These are just fine." I hugged myself to show him how cozy I was.

"Go on now and put these on." He pointed to a cardboard box filled with clothes. He said it friendly enough, but I sensed that I had no choice, especially when he added, "Here, I'll help you."

I shut my eyes as he lifted my shirt over my head, but I knew he kept his open. He unbuttoned my pants and put his hand into my underwear. He pushed my back against the stone cellar wall and pushed two fingers into my privates. I couldn't pretend that I was asleep, the way I did when he laid me down on a blanket or came into my room at night.

I suddenly floated out of my body like a cloud or a spirit, small and nameless, effortlessly indistinguishable. This leaving, my only escape from this dark, smelly place, didn't feel as unusual as it sounds. It was just what I did. I remember rising above my house, and seeing the roof and the chimney, the street with big two- and three-families, the whole city filled with homes and barrooms and sidewalks and cars and people, tiny people going about their business. I stared down and felt able to rest my weary mind. I stopped listening to Daddy's breathing and the sound of our clothes rustling, and the smell of the wet basement.

"Ned!" I heard Mommy scream, as if from far away. "What the hell are you doing?"

I came back to my body in an instant, and Mommy was standing at the top of the bulkhead stairs. She appeared black against the backdrop of sun streaming down the stairwell. Dust motes floated in the air, and I squinted into the harsh light.

Daddy removed his hands from my pants, and I heard his zipper. I wished I were small like those dust motes and I could keep floating. Daddy shoved me toward Mommy. "Stop your screaming, woman."

"Get outside, Rose-Marie!" She leveled a finger at Daddy. "My screaming should be the least of your worries."

A slap was followed by a groan as I reach the top of the stairs. I smelled leaves—wet and earthy—and I lay down on the ground and waited. I felt saved by Mommy, but she hadn't run faster than Daddy. Maybe this was what Jesus felt like when he was put to death on the cross. I wished Mommy were more like Mary, Jesus's mother. Holy and dignified. I wished Mommy was a black bear and I was her cub.

But I knew that by the time she came up the stairs out of the basement, it would somehow be my fault, all of it.

Sure enough, Mommy grabbed my upper arm way too tightly. I heard her crying as she dragged me behind her to the sidewalk.

Cousin Alice was sitting in the front seat and jumped out of the car. "What's wrong, Rose? What happened?" She was holding a bag, and I could smell lasagna and sprinkle cheese. They'd come to bring us lunch. They wanted to feed us. To take care of us.

"I can't talk. Please, put Rose-Marie in the backseat. We need to go now."

Cousin Alice looked down at me and wiped my face with a crumpled tissue she found in her coat pocket.

"How'd you get so dirty?" She looked distraught, and I felt drowsy suddenly. I didn't know what Daddy was doing or how he would finish all that work without me. In some ways, I preferred to stay with him rather than talk. Mommy would demand that

I tell her what happened, and I would whisper it, but the shame would make me sick. And then she'd scream and cry, first with me and then with Daddy. Sometimes, after Mommy would find Daddy and me alone, I would hear them argue; it infuriated me to hear him lie. She would often come back to me, asking if I had told the truth, and become even more upset. Time and again, trying to make sense of the madness.

Daddy, on the other hand, would just act super-sweet toward me.

"Remember; don't tell anyone what we do together," he would murmur.

If I don't say anything, maybe he'll go away.

"Rose-Marie, you know you like it. Don't tell me you don't. You just can't tell anyone. It has to be our secret."

1972

Matrimony of Another Sort

The sacrament of First Holy Communion was more than a simple commemoration of the Last Supper that Jesus had with his disciples. It was also an opportunity for me to pretend that my brother, Peter, and I were getting married. I was eight years old, in the second grade at St. Clement, and he was eleven and attended public school in classrooms intended for children with handicaps, mental or physical. Using the Eucharistic celebration of intimacy to proclaim our love for one another seemed only fitting, as I adored my brother more than anyone I knew.

For most of my childhood, I found sanctuary—whole and absolute—in my relationship with him. He never complained or expressed any jealousy toward me. He never took advantage of me; he was incapable. When I was a baby, he was the one at three years of age, unable to walk, who would tell my mom when I needed my diaper changed or give me a bottle. And anytime he would get sick or need an operation and end up in the hospital—and those times were many—I felt desperately alone and abandoned.

For months leading up to the ceremony, Peter and I would imagine our upcoming wedding. While we practiced at home, Christina and Anna could watch only if they agreed to be flower girls.

"You need to walk side by side," I said sternly.

Anna and Christina moved slow as snails. I'd put strips of tape on the floor, so they could pretend they were coming down the aisle of the church.

Anna suddenly moved quicker than Christina.

"No, no, no, it's as easy as A-B-C." I rolled my eyes. "You can do this! Now, start over."

They moved to the back of the room and began again. Peter stood leaning on his crutches and clapped his hands in excitement.

"Now, one, two, three, and go."

They began pacing down the aisle.

"Great. Keep going. You did it!"

"I don't want to practice anymore," Christina said. "I want to play with your Barbie camper. Can we take it outside?"

"You guys can go. Peter and I need to rehearse the words we have to say before they put the Baby Jesus in our mouth."

"Why does Jesus let everybody eat him?" Christina asked.

"Because he loves us!" I yelled. "You're too young to understand."

"Am not! If he loves us, then how come I can't eat him? I'm hungry!"

"Get her out of here," I told Anna.

I wanted my First Holy Communion to be perfect. When the day finally arrived, the sun shone as bright as a new pin. My whole family, including cousins, aunts, and uncles, filed into church and pretty much filled the front four rows. Christina and Anna kept turning around and waving at the back of the church where Peter and I stood, waiting to make our entrance. I pretended to ignore them, but Peter couldn't help himself and would wave back. Then the moment came.

He walked beside me, one leg in front of the other, using crutches and wearing leg braces made of steel and leather straps wrapped tightly around his atrophied muscles. He was sweating with the exertion and, yet, he was beaming. With each measured step I took beside Peter, in my white dress with silver floral patterns, opaque stockings, and shoes that went clickety-clack, we were approaching that much closer to holy union in matrimony.

The Catholic church premises the sacrament of First Holy Communion on the belief that children who are six and seven enter the "age of reason" and therefore can grasp the meaning of the ritual. I'm not so sure about that. In my mind and in my heart, the Eucharist was truly the body of Jesus. If doing sinful things put distance between God and me, then eating Him was a great way to get close again. I fully bought the idea that God, in the form of a wafer or a sip of wine, could enter my body and become a part of me.

Finally, we reached the altar and knelt laboriously at the rail. The robes that the priest wore swished loudly as he moved about the altar. "Every time you eat this bread and drink this cup, you proclaim your love for Me," the priest said, speaking for God.

My hands were folded in solemn prayer and commitment as I tried to look sideways at Peter.

"This is the body of Christ." The priest held up the small white wafer in front of our faces.

We opened our mouths and made the sign of the cross, saying aloud, "In the name of the Father, Son, and Holy Spirit." Then we walked back to our place at the pews. My knees were sore where I had knelt, yet I enjoyed the texture of the crimson velvet against my skin. I peeled Jesus off the roof of my mouth, savoring the flavor of it. I watched my fellow worshippers walking quietly to their seats or kneeling at the foot of the cross that overlooked the altar. I knew we were all on Calvary seeking redemption for our sins that day. I couldn't imagine what sins my brother might have, but if he was with me, I didn't care.

The splendor of the moment—the candlelight splintering off the gold-plated chalice—was made even more glorious by my imagined matrimony to my brother. Peter and I would always be together; I would keep him safe, and his innocent adulation would shelter me in moments when I felt terrible. The cobalt blue of the stained-glass windows, the emerald green in the sacred paintings, the vivid white of the granite stone that lined the holy pulpit behind which the priest stood, all emanated beauty and significance.

All my prior visits to Sunday Mass—where I constantly absorbed the sights and smells and sounds of Catholic worship—were with me. I believed everything I'd been taught about being good and being rewarded and knowing that it wasn't going to be easy—nothing is easy—but I could hear through the silence, hear the note of God's love in the union. Persevere. Listen from the lowest depths and accept all affliction, my own, my brother's, Jesus Christ's affliction, and then all my doubts will leave.

Afterward, my parents hosted a big party at our house. Nana and all my aunts and uncles and cousins attended the festivities, as was our custom. Huge round platters overstuffed with Italian cold-cuts, olives, pepperoncini, pastries, and sesame-coated rolls filled the dining room table, which Daddy had moved against the wall. The kids sat at a table in the kitchen, and the adults sat in the living room, their plates balanced on their knees. As soon as we were done eating, we begged our parents to let us go outside and play.

"Mommy, can I keep my dress on?" I asked.

"You should take it off or it's going to get ruined," Nana said.

"I promise not to get it dirty, Mommy." I didn't even look at Nana. "Please, let me keep it on. You didn't take Peter's suit off him."

"But he won't get it dirty," Nana said.

"He will, too. He already has sauce on his collar." I didn't really want him to get in trouble, but there was no way I was going to take off my dress.

"Alright, Rose-Marie, go on now and have some fun. I am proud of you," Mommy said, and leaned down to kiss me on the forehead. I knew, even as a little girl, she meant that she was proud of me for receiving my First Communion as much as for making it possible for Peter to be included.

Before going to bed that night, I went into Peter's room and lay beside him. I listened to him drone "Old MacDonald" while he twirled his hair, and then asked him, "Does Jesus know everything?"

"Yup, Jesus is God," he answered, not giving it a second thought.

"Does he know how to make a pizza?" I imagined Jesus wearing a white apron with flour on his face and in his hair. I giggled, and snuggled closer to Peter's dense, still body.

"A course," he said and tousled my hair. "He makes mountains, too."

"Does he know things that Mommy doesn't?" I asked, holding my breath.

"He knows everyting." I heard what he said and felt sick to my stomach. I got out of bed and leaned over to kiss my brother goodnight.

"Jesus wuv you, Rose-Marie. I wuv you, too," he murmured, closed his eyes, and fell fast asleep.

1973

Scruffy

At nine, almost ten years old, I wanted a dog. I'd pleaded for years to get one. I borrowed books from the library about how to take care of them and memorized the text as best I could. One time, I stood on a chair in the kitchen, and, like a prayer, I recited the words about some specific aspect of dog care.

A puppy should be housebroken as soon as possible. When the puppy takes its first water or food, note how long it takes for the puppy to urinate or defecate. When you discover the schedule, take the pup outside when the prescribed time has elapsed after feeding or drinking.

After this recitation, I felt I ought to bless myself, but didn't. Mommy and Daddy looked at each other, and I could see they finally realized the intensity of my yearning as well as how committed I was to taking care of an animal.

We'd had other pets—birds, mostly colorbred canaries, but a few singing ones whose chirping became nearly inaudible as we grew accustomed to their clamor. We had a big, green parrot when we lived in North Carolina, until he tried to fly out of the house through closed patio doors. Christina found him, one wing fluttering and blood coming out of his nose. Mommy put him back in his cage, over which she placed a hand towel. I kept peeking through

Scruffy

the cloth to watch him die. We also had aquariums filled with black mollies, angelfish, and tetras. They looked tiny beside the unrestrained plants that Mommy put in the tank.

At that time, Anna and I were in the habit of collecting strays. There were all kinds of dogs roaming the neighborhood, sometimes alone, sometimes in packs, because there were no leash laws. Sometimes, they'd have collars. Most times, not. Mutts mostly, except for purebred German shepherds and Doberman Pinschers. Anna and I figured out quickly how to get a dog to stick around: we gave them a few slices of bologna or provolone cheese on the back porch. After a while, when it became clear the dog wasn't going to leave, we would ask if it was alright to bring it in the house. Mommy and Daddy allowed us to keep it until the dog officer came by or the owner called. I always got attached more than I should have and would cry for hours after they left.

"We told you the owner was coming, Rose-Marie," Mommy would tell me, rubbing my back as I lay with my face pressed into my pillow.

"I knew the doggie wasn't going to stay, Mommy!" Christina said. "I'm not crying."

"Shut up!" I yelled at Christina. "Get out of here!"

Wanting a dog had become on a par with wanting a life where no one would get hurt without good reason. A life where supper cooking on the stove wasn't just the beginning of counting down the minutes until it wasn't safe anymore. Where getting in a car didn't make me feel sick to my stomach.

We wanted a dog so that we could care for something the way it was supposed to be cared for. A kind of "I'll show you" to the universe. If we could care for an animal, then it would be less apt to lose its way in this life. And if our dog could make it, then maybe we would, too. With just the right amount of love, everything would be all right.

Fortunate Daughter

Mommy started looking for a dog in the classifieds. It took only a few weeks before she noticed the newspaper ad: "Miniature poodles/reasonably priced/available now." It was all we needed to know. Mind you, we weren't poodle types, but Peter, who also loved animals, had a fear of big dogs, probably because if a dog bigger than he turned on him, he wouldn't be able to get away. And he'd had enough experiences of not being able to get away, what with being in a wheelchair and having Daddy for a father.

I didn't care; big or small, I wanted a dog in the worst way.

The night before we went to get our dog, Daddy drove straight home from work, which meant he was sober. Mommy helped me and my siblings make Pillsbury dough pizzas and a tossed salad for supper. We were even allowed ginger ale. Afterward, my parents talked quietly in the kitchen. Mommy washed dishes and Daddy sat cross-legged at the table, smoking a cigarette. He described to her his latest opinions on the Jimmy Hoffa scandal that resulted in a few of Hoffa's men getting injured or killed.

"His old buddies don't want him back. They had themselves a good chuckle over blowing up that there boat."

"It's like my mother says; you sleep with the dog, you get fleas," Mommy said, drying the last pan.

"Or as Hoffa himself would say, 'Rats scratch and bite.'"

The following Saturday morning, Mommy stayed home with Christina and Peter, and Daddy and Anna and I drove north on Route 3 toward Billerica, a suburb of Boston. The rain was falling lightly, and I sat in the front passenger seat beside Daddy. Anna was in the back. I leaned my head against the window. The glass felt smooth and cool on my face. I breathed out warm air and watched it attach to the automotive porthole. I pressed my hand against the glass and scrutinized the pattern of my fingerprints for details about my life yet to come. The car smelled, as always, of cigarette smoke, wet footwear, and motor oil. The radio was on a country station Daddy liked, and Hank Williams was singing the plaintive lyrics of "Never Getting Out of This World Alive."

I hummed along, liking the way the music sounded like someone riding a horse. I still couldn't believe we were on our way to get a dog of our own!

The house was easy to spot. Behind a small, beige-colored ranch on the corner was a large, fenced-in yard filled with dogs of all sizes and shapes. Among them was a poodle, entirely black except for a white patch of fur on his chest that stood out like a shield. All ten pounds of him ran back and forth in front of the gate, but he seemed the most powerful. He barked at us, but he also barked at the other dogs, including the Great Dane, the Collie, and the Airedale Terrier, as if to say, "Back off! Leave those humans alone!"

"Come on, girls," Daddy said, "We're here to see the new pups, remember?"

Anna shrugged and backed up a little. Then she turned and walked toward the house with us. We both had our puddle boots on and giggled at the sucking sound our steps made in the mud.

There was no bell to ring, so we knocked. We heard what sounded like TV and music playing on a radio. Then the door was opened by a large woman with a small child, younger than Anna and me, hanging onto her leg. His brown eyes met mine as the adults introduced themselves to one another.

"You must be the folks who called 'bout Marigold's litter. Come on in." The woman shook Daddy's big hand and moved aside. The hallway was dark, and she led us directly into a kitchen brimming with activity.

A skinny woman cooked bacon at the stove, her hair piled upon her head like a fountain. Two children sprawled on the floor playing jacks, and three tiger-striped cats perched on top of radiators. Four grown men played cards at the table. Some of them smoked ciga-rettes, and all of them were drinking. One of the older men held a stout poodle that was gray as a rain cloud about to burst. While he sipped his beer, the poodle looked up at him.

"My name's Ned, and these two here are my daughters," Daddy said. "You said in the paper you had some poodle pups that you're willing to part with."

"Oh, yeah. Go on. Get the dogs in the parlor," the man holding the fluffy cloud dog said, and the boy who met us at the front door darted out of the kitchen.

"You're welcome to sit down if you can find yourself a chair," the man said. I looked at Anna. We both raised our shoulders like we didn't care. "We're just fine standing," Daddy said, and folded his hands in front of him the way he would if he were singing at church, perfectly still and kind of reverent. As compared to the men in this kitchen, Daddy seemed like a saint, one that would fight the devil and win; he was so strong, so cool.

"You want a beer?" The man held out a beer bottle. "We've got Schlitz or Miller."

"No, thanks," Daddy said, "Too early in the day for me. I wouldn't get a thing done if I started now."

I didn't even try to hide my shock. Daddy, worried about when he started drinking? If I caught Anna's eye, it would feel just like staring into a mirror of befuddlement.

"If you don't want one, then this doggie will have one." He tilted the beer he'd been drinking so it was at nose level of the dog on his lap. She reached her tongue out, and he poured the malted liquid down her throat. And she drank it. Not just a little bit, but the whole bottle.

"She's always liked beer," he said. "About eleven years old. I can remember when she had her first sip, not even a year."

"Yeah, some dogs is like that," Daddy said. "Can't rightly figure it out myself."

Scruffy

The boy returned with a box, not before the little black poodle from the yard came in through the back door. He walked around briskly and came over and sniffed our shoes with authority.

The poodle pups inside the box were the tiniest living furry creatures I'd ever seen. I reached down and picked one up, holding it "snug as a bug" inside the palm of my hand.

"Now be careful not to squeeze them or hold them too long," the little boy said. "They is small enough, my mommy told me, and they can break." He was looking at them like it was the first time he'd seem them. The puppies' eyes didn't open, and their paws were as pink as the brand-new eraser heads on my pencils at school.

"What do you girls think of these young'uns?" Daddy said. "Can you imagine being able to care for something this small?"

The black dog sat beside the box where the rest of the puppies lay sleeping one on top of the other. All of them were pure white and limp like warm, dry dishrags.

"Now, I must tell you we won't be able to let you take 'em home today," the man said. "That is assuming you want one. You'll have to wait a few weeks until they're weaned."

My heart dropped like a rock thrown at random into the water. We weren't getting a dog today? A single tear formed in the corner of my eye, and I brushed it away before anyone could see it.

"We thought the ad said available now," Daddy said.

"That's 'now' in a broad sense." The man made an arching motion with his free hand. The dog in his lap wiggled, learning her head against his chest, and licked him under the chin.

"That's all right," Daddy said, even though it wasn't.

Another man, the one with the big belly and the flannel shirt, looked up. I was holding Anna's hand and placed the puppy I was holding with the other hand back in the box. I didn't want it anymore if I couldn't have it today. I did that a lot, act like it didn't matter that I couldn't have what I wanted.

"Why not let 'em take Charlie?" the woman at the sink said, and the big belly man turned and looked at her. "He's a good dog and grown up enough without being too grown."

"Which one is he?" Daddy asked.

"The one that greeted you when you got here," Big Belly said. "That one sitting beside the new litter. He ain't even the daddy. 'The Boss,' we call him."

The skinny woman yelled over, drying her raw, red hands the way Mommy did, "He's her pup." Pointing to the beer-drinking dog. "One of the nicest dogs I've ever known."

"That's true," Big Belly said. "But we've got ourselves a mess of dogs out back. And these girls want a dog bad. I can see it in their eyes."

I grabbed hold of Anna's hand and bent down toward the black poodle they called Charlie. "Come here, boy," I whispered.

He nudged his cold, wet nose into my hand and allowed me to pet him. I didn't worry that this doggie's mommy was a lush as much as I worried that Daddy was a drunk. His back leg twitched in time with my scratching him under his chin, and he scooted his bottom over so it was next to my leg.

"You girls interested?" Daddy asked.

Anna and I looked at each other and didn't speak, but I knew she was feeling the same as me. I finally said, "He would be fine with us, Daddy."

"Then he's yours," Big Belly said, "and he's cheaper than those miniature white ones you just saw." He paused, looking like he might change his mind. "I don't know what the lot of them in the back will do without him. That's one tough dog. And smart, too."

Anna leaned over and said, "How 'bout Scruffy? Let's call him Scruffy."

He threw up three times in the car on the way home, whimpering softly almost the entire way.

Scruffy

"I want him to sleep in my room, Daddy," I said.

"Now that ain't gonna happen," he said.

I cringed. Of course, he wouldn't want a dog in my room. No matter how nice this day had been, my life would remain my life.

"Where will he sleep, then?" Anna sounded like she thought he'd end up in her room.

"In the back hall. He's lucky we don't put him outside. When I was growing up, we never let animals in the house."

"But he's so little, Daddy, he wouldn't last one night."

"Oh, you'd be surprised what dogs can do. They can handle more than you think, and smart dogs figure out things right quick. I had a dog once who knew where that she-bear was going to come out of the woods well before my daddy saw him coming. Saved his life."

I felt like a dog poised to receive the next dangerous moment with grace and bravery. Would Scruffy help us? Maybe the scales had tipped on our side, but would it be enough? And would I be a good person when all was said and done? I wanted to be, but the space between what I wished for, prayed for, imagined might be possible, and what was happening, grew larger all the time. But there were also days like this.

Winter. Near day's end. A pond frozen over; the snow cleared by hockey skaters. The thermos with hot Lipton tea, super-sweet, just the way Daddy and I liked it. Daddy unloaded a woolen blanket and lugged the sled behind me. Birch trees, bare of their leaves and bent over from the weight of ice on their thin limbs, encircled us.

"Where are we taking the sled?" I asked. "There isn't a hill nearby."

"Haven't you never sledded on the ice?" he asked.

I followed behind. *Daddy should know the answer to that question.* He took out a long, coarse rope and tied it on one end, while I sipped the tea, sugary steam warming my face.

Fortunate Daughter

"Hop on," he said and pointed to the sled. I did as I was told, and he covered me with the blanket. I thought he'd pull me across the ice, not that exciting, but still fun. I felt safe and happy. Instead, he towed me out a ways. Leaving a lot of slack in the rope and walking away from me, he yelled, "Did you put the tea away?"

"Yeah, I left it over there," pointing to the embankment.

"Good," and then he then began. Spinning me, slowly at first, but the rope grew taut as he held tight, knuckles turning white, and turned around and round. The bitter wind rushed against my face and the sun, now a golden shaft of light, shone on everything: Daddy, me, the sled, and the frozen pond.

1974

Easter Sunday

It was 1974. The Symbionese Liberation Army demanded $4 million to release Patti Hearst; I couldn't stop gaping at the black-and-white poster of Mikhail Baryshnikov's face that stared back at me from my bedroom wall; and Anna, sitting at the supper table, could do an impersonation of President Nixon that was spot on.

Dad became less volatile in some ways: cutting down on his drinking and coming home straight from work, acting nice to Mom, and not losing his temper as much. But his new custom, of late, was to punish me for attempting to steer clear of him. Like when I discovered that a necklace he'd given me—with glass beads and fake pearls—was missing.

"Dad, did you take my necklace?" I asked him, fearing that he had.

"What do you think?"

"You did!"

"Then why're you asking me?"

He seemed to be enjoying this game all too much. So I went back to my room and gathered all the presents he'd given me over the years—clothes and jewelry, mostly. I trooped back to the kitchen and dumped it on the floor in front of him. "Here, you can have everything. I don't want any of it."

"You're not done."

"Huh?"

"Get the rest of your gear."

"There's nothing else."

"You're wrong about that."

Oh, shit, what did he mean? I spoke slowly and said, "Just my bed and bureau and desk."

His expression was so cold, I shivered.

"Where will I put it?" I asked.

"That's something you should have thought about before . . . "

"Before what?" I yelled, hot tears streaming down my face.

"Before you stopped . . . "

"Stopped what? Say it!"

He didn't answer.

"Why don't you say it, you coward?"

He stood suddenly and began to take off his belt, but I didn't care. Even though it hurt as he struck me over and over again, I felt like I had won this battle. He could pretend he was being nice all he wanted, but if accepting the gifts obligated me to be his slave, then I didn't want any of those things. At least, that's what I told myself.

A few weeks later, to demonstrate that I meant business, I invited my sisters into my room with the promise that something good was going to happen. I lined up all of my dolls on my bed and told them they could each have—"forever and ever"—whichever one they wanted.

"Go ahead and pick one," I said, waving my arm toward the bed like it was a stage.

Christina reached for the Chrissie doll, who had a ponytail that went up and down and in and out. "I want this one."

"Then I want Shelly," Anna said. "She looks like the sister to Angela."

I made them choose until all the dolls had left my room. My sisters thought I was crazy, but I knew I was done playing with dolls. If I gave away the toys that little girls liked to play with, then I would be more grown up and be more able to defend myself. My attachment to these things made me more vulnerable to him. Giving away my things meant that I was freer of the ways that my dad could control me.

While Peter attended public school, my sisters and I attended the only Catholic school in Massachusetts that boasted twelve grades of Catholic education. By third grade, I knew both their classmates and my own pretty well, as we would see each other on the tar-paved playground, in the quiet hallways, or on the regular routes we would take to and from our homes. When the bell would ring at the school day's end, we lined up in groups according to the direction we would walk: Convent One, Rectory, and Powderhouse. When I got a certain distance from school, I could stop walking in my assigned pair arrangement and move at a more leisurely pace. Girls, more often than not, would turn to chat with one another, and the boys gave themselves over to roughhousing, something they'd been holding back all day until they were like balloons about to burst.

My fourth-grade teacher, Sister Rina, still stands in my mind's eye like an oversized crow in her black wimple, black dress, black stockings, and black shoes. Her hair, the little I could see of it, was gray, but her eyebrows were black. After morning prayers, she addressed the group of thirty or so nine-year-olds to which I belonged:

"Children, I want you to listen to me very carefully. Today, we are going to discuss something of utmost importance." She swept her gaze over us, the way she taught me how to move my paintbrush across paper, in one even motion.

"I want you to think carefully about your answer to this question: Which holiday is more vital to Catholics, Christmas or Easter?" She paused. "I want you to really think about your answer."

Fortunate Daughter

We narrowed our brows and moved our eyes sideways in a desperate attempt to communicate with one another what the correct answer might be, because none of us had any idea.

"Alright, children, on the count of three, I want you to shout out your response . . . one, two, and three!"

Though on some level we must have known we were being set up, we did our best to get it right, and in complete unison yelled, "Christmas!"

Wrong answer. Sister Rina stood perfectly still and clenched the handle of her cane in her right hand as she moved from behind her desk. I feared that she might break it over Jimmy Macaluso's head. I turned to my scrawny friend Joann Ciccarelli and rolled my eyes, though my hands remained folded on my desk and I made certain to keep my feet still.

"Unsuitable, class! Easter is the correct answer. For without Christ's ascension into heaven, there would be no resurrection from the dead and life of the world to come. There would be no Catholic church. Take out your notebooks and write fifty times what you see me writing here on the board: 'Easter is the most important holiday to Catholics. Without Easter, none of us would be here.'"

Easter Sunday. I wore a knee-length, powder-blue polyester dress with a matching belt that tied in the middle. The fabric felt scratchy on my skin, but at ten years old, I didn't care; I enjoyed how the white cotton flowers brushed under my chin when the breeze blew. My stockings were translucent, and my shoes an opaque white with shiny metallic buckles. I carried a purse in a feeble attempt to rise to a level of maturity that I didn't expect my sisters to appreciate. Sometimes, we wore identical outfits, but more often, I purposefully put on something different. They were too young to understand so many things—not like me. I was trying to make sense of masquerade. Rather than spend my life blindsided, I opted to expect betrayal, and I felt scorn for anyone, especially my sisters, when they would get excited or express hope.

Peter wore a bowtie, a cap, and polyester dress pants that fit over his heavy metal braces. Mass began at nine-fifteen, and my parents, being punctual, required us to get there on time.

Easter Mass is typically longer than usual, so my siblings and I were ready to burst out of the church when it ended. St. Clement Church stood on a corner lot on the main street that ran between Somerville and Medford, and was made of big, gray granite stone and giant stained-glass windows. Inside, there were smooth marbled saints, each one in an act of subordination, the smell of recently oiled wooden pews, and the sounds of the altar boys giggling from somewhere behind the altar.

We piled out of the car after Mass, and the strong fragrance of purple hyacinth surprised me, as did pansies in multiple shades of yellow. While I lifted Peter's legs for him, one step at a time up the front stairwell to the second floor, I caught a whiff of the baked ham that Mom and I had covered with mushy pineapple rings and bright-red maraschino cherries held in place with toothpicks and put into the oven before leaving for church.

Scruffy sat under the kitchen table while Dad cut the ham using a new electric knife. We watched the blades buzzing rhythmically through the juicy meat, and our mouths watered.

"That piece is too thick, Mac," Mom said, leaning over, resting her chin on his shoulder.

"Alright, I'll make 'em a little thinner for ya'll." He moved his body so that he could cut at a different angle and bumped into her. She laughed, and her lightheartedness cascaded over us, making us chuckle to see them this way. I wondered if they had acted this way when they visited Washington, D.C., to catch cherry blossoms in full bloom during their courtship. Mom had recently shown us slides of this trip and I could see in their faces how in love they were.

Fortunate Daughter

We were allowed to sneak large pieces of pale, pink meat out of the serving dish, as we had already washed our hands. Even Scruffy got a few morsels that he carried into the pantry to eat. There were also other large pans on the stove: ricotta-filled manicotti, an iceberg lettuce salad with green olives, canned green beans, applesauce, and roasted potatoes. The kitchen was hot, as the oven was on all the time we were at church.

Anna twirled in a patch of sunlight that streamed in through the pantry window, even though she knew she was supposed to be helping. She and Christina both wore ankle-length skirts lined with soft, lacy fringe. Anna's flared open, making it look like a parasol mushroom.

"Anna, stop spinning around and come over here," I said gently.

It was hard for us to sit still through the whole meal. We still felt giddy from waking up to Easter egg baskets filled with milk-chocolate bunnies and bright pink marshmallow Peeps. Dad sat down at the table on time. It was obvious he hadn't been drinking because he was calm, almost enjoying our antics. He and Mom kept smiling, at us and at one another.

Christina got so silly, she slid out of her chair. Dad reached for her under the table and pretended that he couldn't find her. He had our undivided attention, not because we were terrified, but because we loved him. He was our dad, acting like a good dad.

"She's like one of them rabbits that visited us here this morning, isn't she, Peter?"

Peter started to grin and clap his hands. "I almost caught da bunny this morning, Daddy. I weft him carrots and celery nast night and dey were gone dis morning."

"Yeah, but rabbits are a little hard to find once they've gone in their hole." He winked at my brother and Peter clapped even louder with a big grin on his face.

After the meal, we drove to the Fresh Pond reservoir, like many families looking to be outside on a pretty day—but more importantly, a place where we could play and have an Easter egg hunt. It also had walking paths, two playgrounds, hills to climb, and benches to sit on. Dad constantly yearned for the country where he grew up, so this park, minutes from our home, was a place we regularly visited.

That Easter, we were all happy to forget what our "normal" life was like and to believe that good times, however fleeting, meant that maybe there were more good times to come. Things seemed lighter on a day that promised to be bright as sunlight on a stream. In the car, I sat behind Dad. His left arm hung loosely outside the window, and he held the steering wheel with his right hand. The radio played "Love Me Like a Rock" by Paul Simon, and we sang along. I didn't understand why his mother loving him that way made him feel more treasured, but I reveled the melody.

Mom applied fresh lipstick. She used a hand-held mirror to take a peek at us in the backseats as she took out a tissue and pressed down on it with her lips.

"You kids being good back there?" she said, with a smile that warmed me like unclouded sun, and then handed me the lipstick-stained tissue without my having to ask for it. She knew how much I liked the way it smelled and how the shape of her lips resembled a heart.

"Mommy, Rose-Marie thinks she's better than us," Christina yelled. Anna was sandwiched between us. Christina was mad at me. She had wanted to wear my white gloves with small pink roses embroidered on them, and I'd told her she would have to wait until we got to the park before she could have a turn. I also had refused to play house with her and Anna earlier, informing them that I was now too old.

"I do not think I'm better." I said, equally loudly, and reached over and pinched Christina's arm. She winced and straightened her headband, which had dropped low on her forehead. She looked more like a grumpy bulldog than a little girl, and Anna and I laughed. Peter started to laugh, too, and clap his hands again.

Jumping out of the car when we arrived, all three of us helped my brother get into his wheelchair. That way it took less time to get where we wanted to go and do what we wanted to do. I held the basket of hard-boiled colored eggs and asked Mom, "Can I hide them first?"

Christina scowled at me.

Mom put her hand on my shoulder and said, "Yes, as long as you remember to put some within reach of your brother."

I skipped over to the place I wanted to start, at the base of yellow-flowering forsythia branches. Clusters of daffodils poked out through pine needles and damp cedar chips. They stood humble and poised, displaying deep-orange centers surrounded by pastel-blonde petals. I knelt down to put my nose into one of the blossoms and breathed deeply, filling myself with the scent and nearly swooning with delight. I felt deliciously happy and unburdened by my usual fear. It never took very long for any one of us—including me, even though I pretended at times to be impossible to soften—to relax and stop worrying. I secretly hoped that Dad had changed, maybe forever. Also, I believed that if I behaved differently: more faithful, more helpful, and more kind, then maybe my actions would prevent bad things from happening to me and my family.

As I went about the task of concealing my eggs, I bent down and accidentally crushed the delicate petals of crocuses that grew under spruce pine needles: daring and bold, a bordered ensemble of flowers, reaching toward springtime. I wondered if I could be that confident. I also hid a few eggs in the limbs of weeping cherries and crabapples.

Mom yelled over, "Don't forget where you put them, Rose-Marie. You know every year we lose a few."

Easter Sunday

"I know, Mom. I won't forget." I still tasted the sugar in my mouth from the jellybeans we were allowed to eat after dinner.

I looked up and saw Dad go to the car and get a blanket and possibly a bottle of booze—he usually had one stashed under a seat. My stomach flipped, and I bit down hard on my bottom lip. I watched him sneak behind the water-cleaning building and come back after a few minutes, without the blanket. He had a familiar smile on his lips.

I wanted to hide like the bunny we had spoken about earlier. I wanted Mommy to hold my hand and lead me to safety. I wanted to place the eggs in my basket somewhere Daddy wouldn't find them. I wanted to die and be resurrected. I knelt down on my knees and heard Daddy come behind me. He said, "Let me give you a piggy-back ride, and we can hide the rest of these eggs together," in his "Don't refuse me" voice.

So, while my sisters played on the swing set and Mom helped Peter get around, Dad led me away from the normal, happy family life I so wanted to cling to. There were no words spoken as he carried me on his back to a secluded place behind the building where he had just laid the blanket. The silence, heavy and dark as a passing cloud, made it possible for me to ignore the dreadfulness of what was about to happen. If I didn't speak, then maybe he wouldn't be able to use my own words against me later.

He placed me on the blanket like a loaf of bread and, before he sat down, looked for his cigarettes. The scent of tobacco smoke mixed with the aroma of lily of the valley that grew in clusters beneath our blanket.

"Come over here and let me have another look at your pretty dress," he said without looking at me.

I'd been sitting on the farthest side of the blanket, but he moved me closer with one sweep of his arm. I pulled my knees up to my chin. Even though that meant I wasn't sitting like a lady, I felt more protected. The sun shone brightly, and I stared down at my shoes.

Dad rubbed my shoulders and then my back. He pushed me gently so that I lay down with my face in the blanket. He continued to rub my back. I began trying to mentally count where I hid the eggs. I heard him unzip his pants and knew he was touching himself. His other hand slid under my body and searched for my tights and underpants.

I closed my eyes, pressing my face into the blanket.

I imagined myself as one of the silent marble saints that lined the church aisles. Earlier that spring, I'd won first prize for the best Novena essay, which I'd researched at length, looking through the *Lives of Saints*, devouring page after page of various descriptions of martyrdom. I became Maria Goretti, a pious farm girl who at twelve years old was attacked by a nineteen-year-old farm hand. He choked her into submission and then stabbed her fourteen times. She survived in the hospital for two days, forgave him, asked God's forgiveness of him, and died holding a crucifix. While in prison for his crime, he had a vision of Maria where he saw her dressed in white, gathering lilies. She smiled, came near him, and encouraged him to accept an armful of the lilies. As he took them, each lily transformed into a still white flame, and she disappeared.

Dad's breathing changed, becoming slow and deep. I wondered why he wasn't talking. Maybe he'd given up wanting me to answer his constant question, "Does it feel good?" It never crossed my mind to utter the word, "Stop." My fear of outright disobeying him didn't change the sensation of pleasure emanating from between my legs and belly. In one memory, I did nothing to resist the contact and felt destroyed in my silence. In another memory, I held onto my silence as a symbol of my nonagreement. Not speaking permitted me a way out of my moral quandary.

Easter Sunday

"Ned, where are you? I need help with Peter," Mom was yelling, and it sounded as if she were miles and miles away.

Dad moved me off the blanket and adjusted his pants to cover up what he was doing. He took my hand, forgetting the blanket, and walked us back toward the car around the building a different way.

Mom instantly eyed us both and gave me a cold and suspicious stare. "What were you doing up there with Daddy?" I looked down, and Dad released my hand.

"Rose, knock it off. We weren't doing nothing but looking at that there cleaning machine." He said this in a tone that suggested she was crazy for thinking anything else.

"You go with him?" Her whisper an accusation. Dad sauntered off toward where Christina and Anna were playing, and Mom's dark-brown eyes bore a hole right through me. I felt sure she hated me, and I was lost. I remember wishing that I could have carried out my commitment to perfection and that I had, indeed, unearthed some way to leave him. Why couldn't I have spoken? Why wasn't my body more powerful like Maria Goretti's? How would a refusal have changed anything? Why did Mom think that what I did mattered so much?

I knew something about what was going on that Mom didn't. What was I supposed to do? She didn't offer me an example of standing up to him, and I resented her for that, but I also felt like I shouldn't have allowed him to do what he did. In that way, everything she felt toward me seemed true. I was doomed.

Later that night when I felt certain everyone had gone to bed, I snuck out on the back porch in my PJs. The pear tree, tall and reaching, bloomed delicate and beautiful blossoms, sweet to my senses. I looked up at the sky and stared at the scattering of stars. Late-evening quiet, except for some car traffic in the distance and some soft-playing opera music gradually becoming well-defined, the more I strained to listen. It emanated from our Italian neighbors' three-story home across the street. I remembered that my grandfather, Papa, would listen to opera late at night, but no one else I knew did. The song, mournful and despairing, became not mine to listen to, but a continuation of me. My whole world became this music, and still there was not enough of me to hear and understand the words:

Mia madre aveva una povera ancella
Innamorata e bella

The priests staffed the confessionals on Saturdays, so people could request forgiveness for their sins before Sunday services. The organ played in the background, sober and uplifting. My own sins were never difficult to recall. I'd line them up like baby ducks, one in front of the other, and recite them with utter perfection.

The following Saturday, I sat in the shadowy box; sometimes I could see the eyes of the priest through the mesh of the screen. His side was lit; mine wasn't. He didn't need to be hidden; I did. I stared through the grid of our separation. His gaze penetrated me and all my imperfections, much the way Dad looked at me. Knowing all about me. More than I knew myself.

I saw the bottom of the priest's mouth, lips dry as a bone and peeling. He coughed, and I recognized it was Monsignor Hart. I imagined that if I could tell who he was, then he might know who I was. I became filled with a shame that exceeded the knowledge of what I'd done, and I had to remind myself that the mesh acted as a veil.

"Bless me, Father, for I have sinned," I said far too hurriedly. "It has been one week since my last confession. I didn't do all my chores and the ones I finished, I complained about. I stole the Halloween candy out of the Tupperware container my mom keeps hidden in the pantry. I lied about washing my hands before supper. I let my dad touch my private places. I swore at my sister when I knew she could hear me."

Easter Sunday

I spoke rapidly, the words spilling out and the silence in response to what I'd said so quiet it felt loud and longer than I wanted it to be. For a moment, I wondered if the priest was still there, or worse yet, coming to grab me out of my side of the confessional so he could see, really see, the filth that was talking to him. I had no idea— only the church leaders did—the number of priests involved in the recent scandal of priests abusing young children getting relocated to different parishes only to abuse again. My heart pounded the way I imagined a bunny would, knowing she's about to be devoured.

Finally, he asked, "Are you truly sorry for your sins, my daughter?" Without waiting to hear my answer, he said, "Recite three Rosaries, my child, and five Hail Marys."

"Yes, Father." *Did he hear me? Was absolution for my wrongdoings that easy?*

"Go now and repent."

I made the sign of the cross in unison with him, moving my right hand to touch my head, then my belly, and my shoulders, and exited the confessional. When I knelt at the altar to say my prayers, I felt freer and lighter. *Peter must feel this way all the time,* I thought. *Is this what it's like to feel sinless?*

I wondered more about Peter and whether he, too, came into the world with original sin the way the rest of us had. What bad things, I mean *really* bad things, had he done? It seemed only bad things happened to him. Like Jesus, in a way. The nuns told me that Jesus became a man, so God could sacrifice Him. Peter, too, seemed to live on a cross.

Could I live there? I wanted to be like the Jesus at church, with big wings and an uplifted face. I wanted the serenity of knowing that I was on God's side, the right side, and that no matter what ways the world might ignore pain and hypocrisy, I would have faith that things would work out in the end. The Jesus of my childhood didn't grapple with fear or mistrust. He went forward in His life, knowing what to do, even when He felt let down, like the time He asked the apostles to stay awake, the night before his execution. The best I could muster was acting as if I wasn't afraid, even when I was.

Car Rides

Adventure could come in the form of a car ride. Adventure or treachery? That was always the question. Dad parked the station wagon above a trail leading down to a pond he'd discovered north of Somerville. The night before, we'd reset our clocks to one hour ahead and the temperature was cool. The ground was soft and wet beneath our feet, and large leaves of skunk cabbage rose directly out of the earth like emerald green flames. Daddy was taking us fishing.

Water droplets fell from the bare branches over our heads and hit me on my forearms and the bridge of my nose. We made our way down to a good fishing spot, as Dad liked to call it. He carried long, wooden, bamboo poles that rested on his muscular shoulders. I smelled the earth, my bucket abundant with fat, squirming worms. I felt like my stomach was filled with squirming worms as well. These trips were not often what they appeared to be.

Dad did like getting out of the city, that part was true. But mostly, he liked the feeling that being alone with us—with me—gave him. As usual, when I begged Anna to come along, Daddy would give in, but only because we both knew it would do me no good. When he wanted to get me all to himself, he managed time and time again to figure out a way.

So I felt mixed up as we walked down to the pond. I wanted to spend time with him when he wasn't drunk or unhappy. But I hated how helpless these outings made me feel, even with Anna as my watchdog. I enjoyed who we all became when we were in the woods with one another, but I dreaded how he did things to me that ended up making me hate myself!

And I was sure he knew all of this about me, because he could read my mind. That's what it felt like. He knew what I was thinking and feeling all the time, like the priest in the confessional. I could never do anything without him knowing more about me than I wanted anyone to know.

Even though I dreaded what would follow, I rarely considered not taking him up on his offer to take us somewhere. These trips were the only escape we had; our family never went anywhere or did anything outside our home just for fun. We didn't go on vacations. We didn't eat out, and we didn't even see movies. And the places he would choose were often so beautiful.

Dad handed us our poles when we arrived at the water. We stood on the small shore edge and listened and watched, all three of us facing the gentle wind that blew. It was quiet, but in the distance, I heard peepers calling to one another in anticipation of spring. The distant chorus sounded almost like sleigh bells.

"Which one of you can see that there bird?" Dad stood behind us with his arms folded across his chest.

"What kinda bird, Daddy?" Anna asked. "What color is it?"

"Why don't you try looking on your own?" Dad said, and immediately, Anna and I saw it. A great blue heron. It was just about ten yards away, and its gaunt head moved unexpectedly down into the water. When it came up, it had a small-mouth bass in its bill, which it proceeded to swallow whole.

"Yuck!" I said. It was mysterious and disgusting to me all at once.

"Yeah," Dad said, "but if we could catch fish that easy today, we'd be doing something."

Car Rides

"Rose-Marie!" Anna grabbed my hand. "Let's pretend we're married, and I'm the husband and you're the wife. We're standed on an island, and we have to figure out how we can eat."

"You mean stranded. We're stranded on an island," I told her in my "cool" older-sister voice. "How come you get to be the husband?"

"Just 'cuz. Let me this time, and next time you can be."

"Girls, come over here so I can show you what you need to do in order not to starve to death. Your momma wouldn't like if I brought you back all skin and bones." Daddy was trying to keep a twisting worm from getting out of his hand before placing it in a small tin can and wiping his hands on his pants. "Rose-Marie, bring down those cans of sardines and the banana and mayonnaise sandwiches your momma made for us. We may need to eat a little before fishing." He found the thermos of sweet tea. "Are you young'uns hungry now?"

I squatted next to him, savoring the minutes, and unwrapped the food. I listened to his voice and smelled the skunky-egg water. I wished it were warm enough to swim. Anna made me giggle as she heaved a sharpened stick into the water and almost fell in.

After we finished eating, Dad showed us how to attach the worms to our hooks.

"You hook the head of the worm like so, then stretch the worm out and hook the body back on it. That's it, rigging a live worm is that simple." He looked us both in the eye to make sure we were listening. "There is no better way to rig a live worm for fishing."

He then showed us how to cast. "Follow me and I will make you fishers of fish," he said, chuckling. "Some folks can cast a long way, but their accuracy is awful. There may be fish on the right, but they know only how to cast the line to the left. There may be fish on the left, but they keep casting to the right. Casting takes practice."

He allowed us each to take a few turns before leaning against a tree to watch his daughters fishing. He was calm and relaxed, and so were we. The future didn't exist for a while, and I wasn't sure how much time passed before Dad said, "Anna, you stay here. Rose-Marie and I are going to go get us some lures I left back in the car."

I froze.

But Anna was poised to challenge him. She stared at him directly and said, "Daddy, you don't need to go to the car. We've got plenty of lures down here."

He rose off the ground and brushed the leaves and twigs from his backside. At first, it appeared he didn't hear her, and then he said, "Just stay where you are, and we'll be back in not too long."

No discussion. End of story.

He took my small hand, and I went with him. I immediately began to worry that by not fighting back, by not even saying "no," I was betraying my sister, my whole family. I feared what was to come, but I walked passively beside him, not saying a word. Of course, Dad used methods to get around my silence, either by saying that he knew I liked what he did to me or by being more lenient or generous with me than he was with anyone else in our family, as long as I stayed submissive. Leniency and gifts would work on any child, but they were like gold to me—on top of which, it was beguiling to feel pleasure in response to his desire to satisfy me.

When we got to the car, all pretenses disappeared. Dad moved some stuff around in the backseat and spread a blanket. He lay down first and beckoned me with his hand to lie beside him. Initially, his touch was tender, but it became more demanding along with his breathing. The whole time, I kept all my words in my mouth, swallowing them whole, and drifted above my body the way I did when he would enter my room at night.

He touched me all over, focusing first on my yet-to-be developed breasts, and then his hands found the zipper of my pants. I squeezed my eyes shut as he inserted his hands into my pants. Nothing he did hurt, and yet . . . it did, in a way.

"Does this feel good?" he asked.

I didn't answer. I wasn't there. I was looking down at us, watching him in the woods in the car with me, his daughter.

That's when I heard Anna screaming.

"Get out of there! Let Rose-Marie out of the car right now or I'm going to tell Mommy!" She had her face close to the glass and her cheeks were red with fury and embarrassment. "Don't let him do this to you!" I felt so mixed up. When Dad was touching me this way, even though I knew it was wrong, it felt good. Anna seemed so angry, and a part of me knew I should be angry, too. I felt worried for her: I would hate it if Dad hurt her for trying to protect me. It would be my fault, another sin I would feel powerless to wipe away. Another reason to live in shame and doubt, regardless of prayers and talk of a merciful God.

Dad hurried to pull the blankets off us and popped open the back door of the car. He stared at her with a slight grin on his face and said almost nonchalantly, "Who pulled your chain? You've got yourself worked up over nothing. Settle down."

She was pacing like an animal in a cage.

He asked her, "How many fish did you catch?"

She wouldn't answer him. She refused to return to the water without me. I stood near her with my head bowed.

"How come you let Daddy do those things to you?"

"I can't stop him."

"You can. You know you can. I'm telling Mommy."

"Go ahead. I don't care. She never does anything."

"She will. She will this time!"

"No, she won't. She never does."

"It'll be different this time."

"That's what you like to think."

"I'm not going anywhere with you and Daddy ever again!"

She dropped her fishing pole and lunged at me. I slapped her hard on the face, and she pulled my hair. I felt Dad' hands around my ankles as he pulled us apart. He must have heard us hollering at one another and came back to the water. I landed on my knees next to the bucket filled with catfish and looked down into it. Some of the fish were motionless and barely breathing as they stared up at me. Others of them thrashed frantically about. Neither response did them any good.

Another car ride a few months later. We had spent most of the day at Auntie Gina and Uncle Gino's for the annual Memorial Day summer barbecue. Nearly my whole family on Mom's side were there, playing volleyball or swimming in the large above-ground pool. Uncle Gino, big-bellied and loud-mouthed, manned the grill. He and Dad had been drinking all afternoon, and neither gave a second thought to Dad's capability of driving. I never liked Uncle Gino. I didn't even like standing next to him He was a mean giant, always at the ready to squeeze the life out of the little people in the palm of his hand.

"Please put Ned in the back seat," Mom said, teeth clenched, to Uncle Gino.

Christina and I, who had been playing in the lawn sprinkler set up behind the pool, were already in the back seat, still wearing our wet bathing suits and shivering, despite some borrowed and soggy towels that had been thrown over our knees for warmth.

Dad agreed to let Mom drive without much of a fight, and Peter and Anna swiftly moved to the front seat. Either he was too drunk to notice that he had just lost some clout, or he was already scheming the best way to torture us the whole way home. I sat to the left of him in the backseat, as close to the door as possible, and Christina sat on his right. Our 1972 emerald green Mercury Marquis was nothing if not roomy.

My lavender bathing suit was made of thin cotton and secured by a bowtie around my neck. I was eleven and liked how the suit looked on me, even though I'd become increasingly self-conscious about my body. Nearly every day since my breasts became larger and my hips widened, neighborhood men would proposition me on my way to get slush at Tony's, the corner store.

Mom didn't even make it to the end of the street before Dad reached up and began pulling on her long ponytail, still black but now streaked with gray. She hunched forward, but his hands reaching for her again. No one said a word. We were doing our best to move away, in the hopes that he would just fall asleep.

"Where do you think you're taking us?" The pungent odor of booze and cigarettes made me almost gag.

He then looked at me out of the corner of his eye, as if he'd just realized I was beside him. "Where'd you get that pretty bathing suit?"

I closed my eyes and kept my head turned away. Oh, God, please make this end! I don't want anything to happen.

"Why don't you take a nap?" Mom said from the front seat. "We're all tired after a long hot day in the sun. I'll have us home in—"

"Why don't you just shut up?"

And always this memory: He looked at my breasts, then reached his hand up behind my head and tugged on the string that held my bathing suit in place. He loosened the knot and pulled the string to one side. The entire front fell open. He covered my right breast with his left hand and played with my nipple like he was soothing himself from some faraway pain. No one spoke or moved or breathed; Mom turned on the radio to drown out the silence and the sound of Dad's breathing.

ABBA, whose fizzy melodies always gave me a hit of happy juice, came on the radio, but there was no way I could get lost in the lyrics.

Fortunate Daughter

As we drove along, Dad kept fondling me. The setting sun, peeking through the trees, created flashing patterns against my closed eyelids. Mom stopped at a red light, and I opened my eyes briefly and looked over at Christina. She was watching the whole thing with eyes wide open, and I felt doubly mortified.

PART TWO

Heelyng: Middle English origin meaning to make healthy, whole, or sound

■ — ·— ■

More than 88% of adults who were abused as children say they never reported the abuse to authorities (StopItNow.org/guidebooks, 2010), *and nearly two-thirds of all people with diagnosable mental disorders do not seek treatment* (Regier et al., 1993; Kessler et al., 1996). *Stigma surrounding the receipt of mental health treatment, including but not limited to CSA, is among the many barriers that discourage people, especially children, from seeking treatment* (Sussman et al., 1987; Cooper-Patrick et al., 1997).

■ — ·— ■

"When you write, you illuminate what's hidden, and that's a political act."

—Grace Paley

1975

Nantasket

The Vietnam War was ending, the Khmer Rouge captured Phnom Penh, and Jimmy Hoffa went missing. I was eleven years old, and I loved watching TV, especially *The Waltons*, a television show about a 1930s family with eight kids who grew up in the mountains of West Virginia. They had problems, lots of them, but they did their best to get along with integrity and humor and love for one another.

"Wake up," Daddy whispered. "We only have about forty-five minutes."

I sat up and looked at the clock, even though the pull of my dream, the one where I was walking through a large house with no walls and giant windows, tugged at the edge of my conscious mind, urging me to lay down and go back to sleep. Daddy's big hand tenderly stroked my shoulder. And I remembered: We're going to the beach, down to the South Shore.

I jumped out of bed and quickly put on my shorts and a T-shirt. I walked quietly into my sisters' room and went over to Anna's bed. I would have loved it if Christina could join us, but Dad wouldn't let her. Later on, she'd cry about it, I knew that. I felt bad that she felt left out, but there didn't seem a way around it.

"Get up, Anna!" I whispered. "Daddy says it's time to go."

She lay there under a pale blue sheet, awake and pretending to be asleep.

"Please wake up, Anna. I really want to see the sun come up."

"Then go without me." Not opening her eyes.

"No, I don't want to go without you. I don't want to go alone."

"Oh, all right," she said, sounding like one of our old-lady neighbors addressing a child.

I knew she'd be glad she'd come with us. When Dad took us out, we almost always did something out of the ordinary.

The room was still dark, and I enjoyed how things looked almost shapeless in the dim light. We slipped out of our poly-cotton pajamas. The humidity promised another sticky day in Boston. Christina slept, gently sucking her thumb.

"Let's go! Daddy's already outside!" I raced down the front stairs and onto the porch.

We arrive in Nantasket. The top of the sun rose out of the ocean, luminous and pumpkin-orange. Dad leaned his back against the breaker wall and stretched out his long legs. Squatted in front of him, Anna and I, smelling still like pancakes, ran our fingers through the cool sand. The light reached toward us, our cue to run into the sun-kissed ocean. And we did. It didn't matter how cold. The small rocks scraped our shins, our lips turned as purple as grapes, and our hands froze. We might have drowned, the undertow was so strong, but we were free in our bodies.

1976

Finding Ella

I was twelve years old when I met Ella, the first person who helped me—truly helped my whole family—not feel lost and done for. Anna found her. Apparently, she got her name from a woman at an Alateen meeting we'd been attending in the basement of St. Clement Church. Ella worked alongside Dr. Yaffe, a psychiatrist who would soon become renowned for her work in post-traumatic stress disorder. These two self-defined feminists provided individual and group counseling at the Women's Mental Health Collective.

The night before we left for our first appointment, I wrote in my journal:

> *Why did Anna have to tell anyone? How could she? I'll go, but I'm not going to say anything. No one can make me say a word if I don't want to. Daddy thinks it's a joke otherwise he wouldn't allow us to go. I'm not going to go along with him anymore! Not here at home. Not anywhere. Anna is such a fool to think she can do anything to stop him! I hate him! I hate how controlling he is. I hate how Mommy can't do a thing about him.*

After school the next day, Mom brought us to Ella and Dr. Yaffe's office. How she had the wherewithal to arrange these appointments and yet couldn't do more to make our home safe, I will never understand. I also don't really know how Dad, with his incessant need to control our lives, permitted us to talk with these women, so obviously a threat to his reign. Maybe it was because all the earlier efforts to get outside help had fallen flat.

My siblings and I filed in, first Peter in his wheelchair, then me, then Anna and Christina, bringing up the rear position. We did that a lot—fall into our birth order without planning it. It would just happen.

"Welcome, sit where you'd like," a woman with curly brown hair and glasses said to us. The other woman looked kind of like the witch from the *Wizard of Oz*, but I could tell right away she wasn't as mean or scary because of her eyes, gentle and seeing. She stood close to the woman with curly hair, their shoulders touching, and extended her hand, like we were grownups or something.

"I'm Dr. Yaffe, and this is Ella," she said, and they both sat down, Dr. Yaffe gesturing with her hand that we should do the same.

Peter maneuvered his wheelchair into a spot, and my sisters and I just stood there, waiting to be told what to do next.

"You can have a seat," Ella said. "Your parents gave us permission to talk with you. We understand that your family wants help." Pause. "We want to help." And then they looked at each other—not at us—as if to remind themselves or remember. I don't know.

"I need to use the bathroom," Christina said, and Anna and I rolled our eyes in unison.

"Sure," Ella said, and got up to show her where it was. We sat quietly, Peter and Anna and I, looking at the carpet.

"Can I have a piece of paper?" I asked.

"Certainly." Dr. Yaffe moved to tear a piece from the notepad on her lap. Her ankles were thin like willow branches, and I imagined what she'd look like walking in water with bare feet.

"I don't need a big piece, just something my brother can fold. He likes to fold."

"What do you make?" she asked Peter, handing him a piece of torn notebook paper.

"He doesn't make anything," I said. "He just likes folding."

My sisters and I sat on the soft, large couch, our knees touching. I felt enveloped by worn and textured corduroy. Cocooned within the warmth, my breath deepened, and my eyelids closed, as my sisters simultaneously raced to answer Ella and Dr. Yaffe's questions.

"So, you're telling me that even though he hits everyone in the family, it's mostly you, Anna, whom he goes after the most?" Dr. Yaffe asked.

"Uh-uh," Christina said. "He hits Mommy the most of all."

"She's asking us about what Daddy does to us kids," Anna clarified. "I caught him looking through the keyhole when I was opening the bathroom door. He got a big egg on his head."

I pretended to listen, so as not to alert anyone to the ringing in my ears, the ringing that blocked out everything and separated me from the "what" that was going on outside of me, the ringing that prompted me to realize something was happening that made me feel like my life as I knew it was over, that I was going to die, at least the "I" that existed before the sound.

In any case, Ella and Dr. Yaffe made recommendations for the course of therapy they thought would work best for our family. My sisters and I now were now required to see Ella separately. I wouldn't be able to sleep through one-on-ones.

I wrote in my diary:

Will Ella help me? Is it possible to be honest with someone and have it lead to good? What might Ella accomplish that no one else has? Does she have that kind of power? Do I have the patience? Maybe I should have prayed more. Isn't that what Esther wondered. I'd rather be with her now in Siberia. With Esther from the Endless Steppe.

Fortunate Daughter

■ - — - ■

It was the middle of the week, and after a snack of fruit cocktail, Mom drove me over to Ella's office. Still wearing my school uniform, my backpack felt heavy on my shoulders, as I had a lot of homework. Most of the buildings in that area looked run-down and neglected; her office sat above an abandoned storefront on a main street in Union Square, Somerville. I stepped cautiously into a first-floor doorway, half expecting someone to scold me.

The sweet, greasy aroma of General Tao's chicken and shrimp fried rice wafted up from the Chinese restaurant next door. Ella sat in a chair opposite mine, a dark-skinned white woman with a warm smile, wearing a long gingham dress and Birkenstock sandals. This was not the way my family dressed, nor was it the way most of the people in my school or neighborhood dressed.

Notepad on her lap, pen in hand, she smiled what appeared a practiced but also genuine smile. I was good at knowing the difference.

"Rose-Marie, do you know why you're coming here?"

"Sort of."

"Your family has been in crisis for a long time now. On some level, your parents—your mom, at least—want to set things right."

"Sure, she does."

"You don't believe her?"

"Would you?"

"Do you believe I can help you?"

"I don't know. Nobody ever has."

"Has anyone ever tried?"

"Well, Auntie Gina offered to take us."

"What happened?"

"We didn't want to go. It's not like Uncle Gino is that much better."

"Than whom?"

"My dad," *Who did she think I meant? Adults were so clueless sometimes.*

"Would they have taken all of you?"

"No, that was the other problem. Some of us would have stayed home, and none of us wanted that."

"What would you like to be different in your family?"

I never liked that question. There were so many things I wanted to be different. And I really didn't like the way someone who didn't live with me, with my family, could come along and make it seem like they could make everything better when I knew they couldn't.

"What are you thinking?"

"About taking Scruffy for a walk this past weekend."

"It was a nice weekend?"

"Yeah, you could call it that."

"What happened?"

"Scruffy ran away. And we had to spend a long time looking for him. Eventually, he found us. I thought he was gone. If I had the choice, I don't know that I'd come back."

"Why?"

"Because Dad is a liar."

"What does he lie about?"

"Everything. And he tells me things he shouldn't."

"Why do you think he does that?"

"I don't know. He likes to feel important."

"Did anything else happen when you took Scruffy for a walk?"

How did she know? What was she writing? How come she didn't have a tape recorder? Could she listen to me and write at the same time? Did other people, like that doctor woman, read her notes?

I left the appointment, and I felt lighter for the first time in a long time. Nothing had changed, but the possibility that something might seemed more probable. I sat outside Ella's office, waiting for Mom to return, and my heart raced so hard, I thought it might burst out of me. I'd been reading *The Guinness Book of World Records* with Anna and Christina sitting beside me, and I knew stranger things could happen.

Maybe my family is more like Ella's family than I realized. Maybe I will survive and have my family, or some part of my family, to lean on. Maybe that will get me through.

"I'm sorry I kept you waiting. My daughter's babysitter needed a a ride home," Ella said breathily, as she opened the door into the waiting room where I'd sit each week. I'd been seeing her for a while by then, and it wasn't unusual for her to be late.

I didn't mind, really; she was an adult woman in my life trying to help me. She settled into her seat, and the diamond from her gold engagement ring reflected light into my eyes for a split second, causing me to squint. I settled into my seat, knocked my knees together, and moved my hand along the edge of the arm of my chair.

"What do you want to talk about today?"

"Nothing."

"May I suggest something?"

"Okay . . . "

"Do you remember the first time your dad touched you in a sexual way?"

"No," I said, but I did. I went into my parent's bedroom to wake up Dad to go to work. We still lived in North Carolina, so I must have been about five years old.

She saw the memory surface. I was used to her doing that.

"What parts of your body did he touch?" she asked me slowly. Her feet were planted on the floor in front of her. I wondered if she bought her sandals in Harvard Square, the place where all the hippy freaks bought their shoes. But I didn't ask.

I whispered, "My chest." The words that fell from my mouth hung like icicles, tapering and cold.

"What did you say?" she said. "I couldn't hear you."

I had to say it again. "My chest. He touches my chest." I paused and kept my head down.

"Anywhere else?" she asked.

"My . . . private parts," I mumbled, praying she wouldn't make me say it again. My hands were clenched into fists and rolled under my thighs. My heart pounded like the gong of a bell. Maybe she would hear it and stop torturing me.

The night before, I'd prayed a whole rosary on my knees beside my bed. When I prayed, I didn't have to say what I let Dad do. God knew, and God forgave me. God knew everything. And that made me feel better. My God was a just God, and Dad would get his due. Besides, prayer always resulted in my feeling better. Not like seeing Ella. Sometimes I'd feel worse for days.

"With what parts of his body?" she asked. She always looked at me when she spoke, even when I didn't. But her eyes were never angry. And she never acted surprised by what I said. "I know this must be hard for you, Rose-Marie. I appreciate your courage for telling me things you may never have told anyone."

How did she know? Maybe she was like Dad and could read my mind. I didn't have any privacy. Not from God. Not from Dad. Not from Ella. I felt completely isolated most of the time, and yet I never had any solitude. Like a prisoner in a holding cell, I was completely by myself, but always under the constant surveillance of Dad's gaze.

"Mostly, his hands," I said quietly. "Sometimes his face."

"Can you tell me a story of when he does this?"

"Every time he would take us for a walk, he would offer to carry me on his back. But when I climbed up, he always put his fingers in my . . . " I couldn't say it, even though I knew Ella wanted me to say it out loud, to put outside what I'd been thinking on the inside, so it would stop eating me up, making me feel ashamed and isolated.

"Did he ever ask you to put his penis in your mouth?"

Yuck! How could she say that?

"No, definitely not," I said, feeling glad that I could finally deny something. Dad had never raped me or put his penis in my bum. I knew men could do those things, and sometimes, I wished he had. It would make it clearer, less weird. The sexual things he did to me were not physically painful; they did not hurt me. If anything, because it felt good to have him touch me, I didn't know what category to put my suffering in. It felt dirty in this way that exaggerated my predicament.

Maybe I disappeared into my thoughts for a few minutes, thinking of how often I had lay awake, staring at the wall that joined me to my parents' bedroom, waiting for Dad to move toward me. When he arrived, I'd pretend I was asleep, eyes closed, my breathing deep and controlled. He'd enter the room quietly. In our home, none of us could close our doors, let alone put locks on them. I had a sheet, two or three blankets, and a quilt that Nana had crocheted for me covering my body. And I always wore pajamas. As my body developed, I learned to leave on my bra, and sometimes my clothes, over my pajamas. I wanted as many layers as possible between his hands and my body. He smelled of cigarettes and alcohol, his touch gentle. He didn't ever speak, but his own breath deepened and sped up as he moved his hands over my body.

Or maybe I looked out the window and saw a child with her mother crossing the street, and the child took her mother's hand, to feel less afraid, and the mother looked both ways before looking down at her daughter to signal that it was safe.

I could have. I could have, also, been thinking again about Auntie Gina's offer to have my sisters and me move in with her family. I don't know what incident prompted this offer, but it was genuine. Ironically, living with Auntie Gina would have its own hazards, possibly the same ones and a few more. Uncle Gino was no saint. He scared me, everything about him: his size, the way he talked, how he never looked at the person he was talking to, even his own kids.

Ella's questions were grueling, but the thought of not coming was out of the question. Besides, I had started to piece together the life she led outside her relationship with me, even though it wasn't easy. I knew these things: She was married to a nice man; she had children; she lived in Cambridge, in one of those big houses built a long time ago; and she was a hippie, or at least she had been. She dressed beautifully, always in fabrics that were soft and richly colored, cobalt blues, burgundy reds, emerald greens. When something was funny, she laughed with delight, like she'd been able to laugh her whole life. When she listened to my stories, she would ask questions to clarify where they fit into the larger story. Was that what she was doing? Piecing together my story? Was that what she did? Compare it to other stories she heard or read about? Did she ever weigh my childhood against her own? To how she raised her children? Did she understand what I told her? How could she, unless she, too, was abused? If she did understand me, what I was telling her, how did she decide what to do about it?

One afternoon, Ella said, "Let's talk today about a more recent incident where your dad touched you in your privates." She rarely used the word abuse. She knew that if she put a label on anything, it would dramatically skew what I told her.

"From when?"

"You choose."

I knew immediately what I wanted to tell her but didn't say anything. I wavered constantly about how much to share. The place she seemed to be leading me felt as unapproachable as a star.

But I had forgotten how perceptive she was. "What did you just remember?"

"Nothing," I said.

She waited.

"We were all sitting on the sofa watching *Star Trek*, and Dad came in after supper. He made us all move down so I would be the only one sitting next to him."

"Did you know he was up to something?"

"Yeah, but Christina didn't. She got mad 'cuz she felt left out. Anna knew, though. She went and sat with Peter in a huff. I wanted her to come back, 'cuz sometimes we could get Daddy to tell us a story and he'd forget why he sat next to me in the first place."

"What happened then?" Ella asked.

"He threw a blanket over us and that's when I knew what he was going to do. When he thought no one was watching his hands, he touched my thigh and then I felt his fingers at the zipper on my pants. He tugged and then reached into the tops of my jeans without bothering to unzip them. He touched my privates, and I closed my eyes and didn't say a word." And it felt good, I didn't say. Besides, he would be mean to me if I didn't let him have his way.

"Then what happened?"

"Mom came in the room to see if any of us wanted a Popsicle and screamed at me and Dad. Before he could answer, Christina, who'd also left the couch to go sit with my brother, ran from across the room. She kicked me full in the face. Blood gushed out of my bottom lip. I covered my mouth and tried to stand up."

"How'd you feel?"

"I was confused and surprised and hurt, but it felt kind of good, too."

"Why good?"

"She knew what Dad was doing, and that it wasn't right. I agree. I don't care that I was the one she hurt. At least it made him feel embarrassed."

"What happened then?"

"Dad jumped up and reached for his belt, and Mom screamed, 'Don't you dare hit her! She knew you were up to no good!' Blood was coming out of my mouth and spreading across the floor.

I caught Christina's eye, and she smiled back at me. She knew I wasn't mad at her."

My palms were sweaty, and my mouth was dry by this point. I forced myself to look at Ella, fearing that once I told her these things, she would realize what a mistake she made in trying to help me.

"What did you tell yourself about what happened?"

"I shouldn't have let Dad touch me. Christina was right to be so mad at me."

"How about now?"

"I told you. I shouldn't have let it happen."

"You're not responsible for what happens to you, Rose-Marie. You are a child. Your parents are in charge."

"That's not true!" If I believed her, then I'd have to blame my parents, and that would be worse.

"What did your dad tell you after every incident?"

"He'd tell me I liked it, and then he'd tell me I couldn't tell anybody else."

"He told you that because he didn't take responsibility for what he was doing, Rose-Marie. He's the adult; you're the child. It doesn't matter that it felt good or you didn't do more to get away. It wasn't your fault."

"It was my fault. I let him do those things to me. I could have done more to stop him. I could have done more to feel differently."

"Our bodies don't judge their sensations. They aren't like our minds that way. We have no choice about how we feel. Besides, it seems like the only time your dad was tender was when he abused you. That's why other members of your family are jealous. You've been put in an impossible circumstance. But you don't have to stay there."

She didn't get it. Blaming me was the only way out. I couldn't rely on anyone else. I could only rely on myself.

"You don't have to be alone anymore, Rose-Marie. You're not alone."

"I am." I held to this belief tight as a whistle.

"Look at me. I will always be there for you. You will always have me on your side. You can always call me, and I will always come."

I was crying now.

"What's making you cry?"

"What you're saying. It can't be true."

"Why not?"

"Nobody can protect me. No one ever has. No one ever will."

"I am going to help your family. I will do everything in my power to ensure that your dad never abuses you again."

She smiled warmly, and it felt as if she touched me. I realized that I had no choice. Even though I wished I had a different life to describe to her, one with nicer problems, I made the choice to tell her everything, to be honest, including, especially, the parts that made me feel mortified. The parts that made me feel ashamed. If I was going to get out of the mess, I had no choice but to trust her. I understood that I had to tell her what happened to me, what was happening to us, and how I felt about it. I had to remember and share with her what I remembered to understand myself.

1977

Wallpaper World

I sat looking out from the second-floor living room. The breeze that blew in the newly opened windows was warm, and the sky was dark with rain-filled clouds. Scraps of ice in the shadows of the sidewalk gutters reminded me of winter's recent passing. I'd been seeing Ella for nearly two years, and things had changed, but not everything. And not enough.

March, 1977. Jimmy Carter was president, Mom couldn't stop listening to Luciano Pavarotti, and I was trying to figure out a way to see *Saturday Night Fever* without my parents finding out. An ordinary Saturday morning. Christina and Anna were upstairs using the Viewmaster we got for Christmas; the color TV was on in the living room, and Peter was watching Scooby Doo cartoons while building abstract LEGO structures in red, white, and blue.

I was thirteen years old, decked out in white bell-bottoms and a navy-blue sweatshirt, blasting music out of the radio. "Hotel California" was playing.

I loved this Eagles' song but couldn't figure out for the life of me what it was really about. It had been difficult for me to distinguish between heaven and hell, and the song didn't help.

My parents moved around the house quickly as they went about preparing for a "day of chores." The value they both placed on work determined the tempo of every weekend.

Fortunate Daughter

Dad was still a long-legged, burly man who worked long hours as a union member truck driver for Integrity Extreme, a local food supplier. His idea of leisure was looking for horse manure to fertilize tomato plants that we'd plant in our small yard in June. On such outings, my sisters and I would follow behind as he entered woods that he knew had horse trails. We'd fill our buckets with piles of fresh "pucky" to shovel into the eight-inch holes that lined our back fence. It embarrassed me to admit how much pride I took in collecting poop.

Sitting at the kitchen table that Saturday, Dad announced abruptly, "We're going to wallpaper Rose-Marie's bedroom!"

I felt the familiar ambivalence. On the one hand, the paint in my room was dull and peeling, and I wanted so badly to fix it up just like the bedrooms I'd seen in home improvement catalogs. On the other hand, I felt scared. Often, when Dad began the day with plans like this one, they ended up costing the rest of us more than we bargained.

"How 'bout Rose-Marie and I head on over to Wallpaper World later this morning?" he told Mom, pretending he was asking a question.

"Oh, Ned, do we have to do that today? Maybe we could do a food shop instead. The girls have been busy all morning, and I'm not up for it."

Her back was turned to us as she washed the pots from last night's manicotti. She wore bright pink rubber gloves that made her fingers look bigger than they were. She was already on edge and trying to hold ground with the charade that they were the sort of couple who discussed their plans and decided together what made the best sense for their family. Not that I knew any of these couples. Auntie Ada and Uncle Leo weren't like that. Auntie Gina and Uncle Gino certainly weren't. Cousin Alice and Cousin Vico—no way!

She was right about us being busy, too; we'd already made our beds, cleaned the bathroom, vacuumed the entire house, mopped the kitchen floor, washed the car, and watered all Mom's houseplants. I now sat at the kitchen table eating a peanut butter fluff sandwich on Wonder bread. I glanced at the *TV Guide*. On the cover was a picture of my two current superheroes, Wonder Woman and the Bionic Woman. The Bionic Woman wasn't really a superhero, but she was beautiful and smart. I conscientiously looked *TV Guide* over every week, planning out my evening schedule according to my favorite shows. Tonight, I was hoping I could watch the new *Starsky and Hutch* episode, where Hutch was supposed to crumble in the face of yet another relationship breakup, and Starsky needed to remind him who he really was. I loved these stories the best because they made me cry, something I wanted to do a lot more than I did, and the excuse of feeling something for a TV character made it less conspicuous.

"Oh, quit your bellyaching!" Dad said. "Rose-Marie has wanted to decorate her goddamn bedroom for months now!" Putting it all on me.

Mom took her cue. "Alright, but could you get a few things at Johnnie's while you're out? We need some bread and sandwich meat before we start the week."

I wished Mom would just stand up to him. I loathed her for so many things, including letting him tell her what to do and how to do it all the time. I decided I would never be anyone's wife or mother when I grew up. I wanted to be a nun and live a free existence, living only with women who got to travel around the world and go to college and teach young children how to "act like they have some sense."

In sixth grade, I had listened each week to the fabulous stories that Sister Marion Louise told the class about her own assignments around the world, and the way it seemed she could decide what she wanted to do and when she wanted to do it. Many people assumed nuns to lead solitary lives with little or no pleasure, but I knew better. The nuns who had been my teachers were all full of gusto, wit, and appetite for life. I savored the fantasy of living without restraint or fear, and I grasped that a life without men as central to one's survival might be a life less terrifying.

Dad slipped on his heel-worn work boots and looked for his wallet. I grabbed my jacket and hurried down the back stairs. I waited outside for him to come down, leaning against the carrot-colored Bronco parked in front of the house. I was resigned to my role as chaperone, even though I couldn't stand how much control he had over us. I was also aware that Mom always seemed relieved to have him gone for a few hours. I resented her for sacrificing me to him this way, again and again.

Liana, the youngest daughter of a large Italian family who lived across the street from us, came over. My sisters and I were pretty good friends with her and her older twin sisters, Lilly and Cathy. Sometimes we'd play a game, but mostly all of us enjoyed getting away from our parents together. I'd been inside their house only a few times, and the last time their father, Tony, belted them so badly that blood—their blood—was all over the floor of their bedroom. That morning, Liana had been playing "Two Square" with her brother, Rocky, and she was looking for an excuse to stop, as he kept slamming the ball into her, acting like he didn't mean it and then raising his hands over his head Rocky-like, as if he'd become more important by bullying his little sister.

"You guys coming out today?" Liana asked.

"Nah, my parents are making us work," I said, knowing she'd understand.

"I hear ya. Can I go play in the fort?"

We had built a fort in our backyard a few weeks earlier out of old wooden pallets we'd found behind the A&P, and she didn't feel comfortable going in there without one of us with her.

"Uh-huh, but my dad says it's not stable," I said, not wanting her to get hurt. She was about four years younger than me, but I liked her the most of anyone in her family. She was the youngest of seven and, like a lot of runts, full of curiosity and nerve.

"Shit, I ain't got nothing else to do," she said. "If I go in, Ma is gonna make me hang the laundry."

"Why don't you go down to Tony's (the corner store owned and operated by her dad). At least you can hang out and get some slush?" Liana didn't have to explain her desire to stay outside; I knew lingering in the street was an effort to endure her status as the youngest female in a home where she was likely to be either ignored or assailed by boorish exchanges.

It was 11:00 a.m. when Dad and I drove toward Wallpaper World. Dad was happy to be out of the house and alone with me. He also seemed to genuinely like the idea of fixing up my room. I didn't feel particularly worried that he was going to take me somewhere where he could abuse me. That would have been too obvious in broad daylight, although there'd been times when the time of day didn't matter.

We entered the large warehouse, which was filled with aisle after aisle of giant rolls of wallpaper stacked ten feet high—every color imaginable and patterns I had never dreamed of. I laughed out loud when I saw wallpaper covered in a fake velvet pimp hat print. Other shelves were filled with buckets of paste, brushes, and rollers. The place smelled both sweet and toxic; I took big whiffs just like I did at the filling station, as I strolled between the aisles. The wooden floorboards creaked below my feet, and I became lost in the warmth and darkness. I touched some of the wallpaper covered in pink polka dots and yellow peace signs.

Dad chatted with the store owner in a relaxed sort of way. Was he faking it, or did he truly feel at ease here? I didn't know. There was a lot I didn't understand or even want to know about him. Like what made him howl all night in the attic after getting drunk and scaring all of us.

"You should go there around the end of May," Dad was saying. "That's when the alewife run. And there's oodles of them." He was telling the store owner about the fish at Sandy Pond in Melrose. The store owner seemed to enjoy the conversation, but what did I know? He also knew my dad was going to spend some money.

"You can reach down into the water with your hand and come up with a fistful." Dad looked up and said to me, "Did you find something you like?"

"I did." I went over to where I'd found some flowered wallpaper, violet blossoming roses opening their petals in various stages of growth, surrounded by pea green leaves. He bought what he thought would be enough for my small room and told the store owner he'd return to buy more another time.

"We'll probably do my son's room next month," he said, leaving the store with me walking beside him. I carried the wallpaper, and he had the buckets, brushes, and glue.

When we got in the car, Dad immediately told me he needed to make one stop before going to get the groceries. My heart dropped. Sure enough, five minutes later, we pulled up in front of a small neighborhood bar. I stayed in the car; I'd gone into bars with him before and didn't like it one bit! Everything about the day that had seemed promising was stamped out.

After what seemed like a long time, Dad jumped back in the car and drove a short while before stopping at another bar. (At that time, Somerville had more bars per square mile than any other city in Massachusetts.) This time, he told me to come in with him.

"I'll just wait."

"No, you won't. Now get out of the damned car."

I knew if I didn't do what he told me, he'd backhand me right there and then—or wait until we got home and do something worse.

It was early afternoon by then, and I could barely see anything as my eyes adjusted to the dark. I knew I didn't belong there. A few men sat at the chrome-fringed bar. They were of varying ages, but mostly as old as or older than Dad, talking in whispers and hunched over their drinks. Dad motioned me to sit next to him. I felt awkward and embarrassed to be there, but no one said anything.

The bartender asked Dad what he wanted, and then looked at me.

Dad said, "Tell the man what you want, Rose-Marie." He was well into the start of a buzz and his mood was light and friendly. He acted like he really cared.

"A ginger ale, please," I whispered.

The bartender smiled and brought us our drinks. Dad swallowed his—a shot of Jack Daniels—and followed it quickly with a beer. As he placed his glass on the countertop, he motioned for a second round. He drank like he was dehydrated—fast and without thinking. When he was done, he paid the bartender and we left. When we got back to the car, he told me to wait for him because he had one more errand to run. I shook my head and didn't say anything as we drove to a liquor store.

Sometimes on these excursions, he would leave me alone for more than an hour, and I had to decide whether to wait for him, go and get him, or walk home. I had never left him, but the idea was always so appealing.

I shoved my hands into my jacket pockets. When I exhaled, I could see my breath. My nose was cold, too. I felt more afraid as each moment passed, and I wished I were home with my family or in the backyard with Liana in our fort. We'd be lying beside each other in the darkness, making each other laugh or planning a trip to Italy. I bet the rest of my family was glad that Dad was out of the house, and I felt a burst of jealousy and rage so large, I pounded my thighs with clenched fists until I couldn't anymore.

Fortunate Daughter

Just when I thought Dad wasn't coming back, he jumped into the driver's seat, casually throwing a bag of glass bottles into my lap. He was in his "I don't have to answer to anyone" mood and drinking a can of Fresca swiftly as we headed toward home.

"Wanna sip?" His words slurred, and he placed the can too near my face.

"No, Dad, you know I don't like that kind of drink." I stared down at my dull-brown orthopedic shoes and sat on my hands. I could easily guess what the rest of the day would be like, but there wasn't anything I could do to change the course of events. I began to feel like my body was enlarging as my terror expanded inside of me. We'd been gone a long time. I wondered if Mommy felt worried about me or was relieved to have us gone still. And we hadn't even stopped to pick up the groceries.

When Dad parked the car, at the A&P this time, he handed me a twenty and told me to go in the store by myself. He seemed to recognize that it would be too hard for him, his mood gloomy and foreboding. I noticed now that his eyelids drooped heavily, and his bottom lip protruded generously from his unshaven face. He looked like a basset hound, but I didn't feel the sympathy I would for a dog. A dog is loyal and gentle, like Scruffy. Dad was more like a bomb ticking on the seat beside me.

I moved quickly in the store, thinking the faster I moved, the less he would be able to drink. When I returned to the car, he demanded I drink from the can again. It was less full, so I agreed. After a cautious sip, I realized he had spiked it.

"Dad, you put something in this!"

"Don't yell at me, young lady. Drink it or I'll make you walk."

I pretended to swallow the bitter, bubbly liquid, and the rest of our ride was silent. I bit my bottom lip and tasted blood in my mouth.

When we got back to the house, everything was quiet except for the murmur of the television as we climbed the stairs to the second floor. Things seemed so calm and yet, Mom and my siblings must have known that we were gone way too long. Anna and Christina and Peter were in the living room watching *Creature Double Feature*. I heard the roar of Rodan, a giant, overprotective female turtle, and smiled to myself. Mom came out of the bedroom. Her hair was mussed up and her cheeks were flushed. She had been taking a nap. I looked at her angrily, and Dad and I brought in the groceries. I left the wallpaper stuff in the front hall.

"Alright, you kids. Get off your asses. We're going to do some home decorating."

Dad was talking way too loud, and he glared at us as if we were giving him an argument. I never understood why he looked like that before any of us had said anything to suggest our lack of submission. Now we were the dogs, waiting to be kicked. I wished I could be like Scruffy, who was pacing with his small, furry chest puffed out. He was ready for whatever would follow, and I rubbed his small head a little too hard. He licked my fingers and whimpered.

Mom suggested that Anna and I work with Dad for a little while, and she'd call us when supper was ready. She was strategizing how best to appease him. If we all did exactly what we were supposed to do, maybe he'd eat dinner, get tired, and fall asleep. I tried to let my thoughts wander. I pictured myself going up and punching him in the face until he cowered. I pretended I was Rodan, flying down to my family and removing Dad with sharp claws.

Anna and I cleared all the furniture out of my bedroom, but the old wallpaper needed to be removed. Dad assigned Anna a spot across from me. She was to work on the bottom half of the walls, and I was to work on the top half. I climbed up on the ladder.

He sang the lyrics from an old Roger Miller tune quietly at first and then belted out, "ain't got no cigarettes," like there was no tomorrow.

Then it began. He yelled at Anna full volume, knowing she would be the one most likely to react. "You're holding the scraper the wrong way! Can't you do anything right?"

I faced the wall and said nothing. As the parched sheets of old wallpaper started to fall, I felt my heart breaking. I imagined writing a message on the walls that would someday be found by somebody. *He yells at us all the time and he hits Mom when he thinks no one can see him and he kicks our dog and he doesn't allow us to play at other kids' houses and he pretends he's gonna change and he touches me in places he's not supposed to.* The list would go on and on.

"When I was a kid, we didn't have anyone to teach us how to do a thing, and that didn't make it so we did as lousy a job as you're doing!"

My knees were shaking as I scraped, pretending I wasn't in the room with a mad man.

"You don't know what you're doing! You haven't got a clue!" He shoved Anna out of the way in his effort to demonstrate his technique.

She turned to face him. Her right cheek was ablaze with a ruddiness that only appeared when she was about to do something without thinking first. Before I could say anything, something to deescalate the situation, she challenged him outright.

"Leave me alone!" she screamed up into his face.

I was so proud of her, but at the same time, I thought she was incredibly stupid.

"Who do you think you're talking to like that?" He began to remove his belt.

"Dad, why don't you let her just do what you asked," I said quickly, even though I knew it was too late. "And she promises she won't say another thing. Right, Anna?"

She stood there motionless, wordless. Saying everything and

nothing at all. She had one second to tell him that she'd do what he wanted, and then that second was gone.

I turned back to the wall I was facing, deciding not to watch. From the sounds of it, I knew he was hitting her everywhere—her face, her arms, her back. The room wasn't big, and she had nowhere to hide. I heard her scream and hit the wall repeatedly, but I didn't turn to watch or do anything to help. This could have been the day I decided she'd brought it on herself, just like Mom. She knew how far to push it, and she went past that point. Salty tears reminded me that I, too, needed to remember my place in this house, in this world.

Anna was begging now, but he didn't stop. He pushed her while he was thrashing her. I heard her head slam hard against the wall, and I winced. He pressed her face into the wall and dragged it across like it was a paintbrush. I turned then and saw a solid trail of blood, and I yelled, "Look, Dad! She's bleeding! Stop!"

He noticed it, too, and shook his head like a horse bothered by flies. Suddenly, he laughed like a hyena and let go of Anna's face. She slumped to the floor and appeared in a trance.

I descended from the safety of my ladder perch, and he said to me, "Don't move. You're not going anywhere!"

I heard Mom now on the other side of the door, which he'd locked when we went into the room. She'd apparently been shouting his name, over and over, for some time. Dad dipped one of the paintbrushes into a bucket of primer and, without shaking off any of the excess paint, tried to paint over the blood on the wall.

I made my way to the door. Dad painted methodically and continued to laugh a small chuckle. I knew I had to get out, but I wasn't leaving Anna.

"Do you want some food, Dad?" I asked him, removing any hint of insolence from my words by long practice. "How 'bout a cigarette?"

He was looking through me and searching in his pockets for something. I reached down and took Anna's hand. She leaned against the wall for support and held my fingers tightly.

He found some matches and was looking for his cigarettes. "Let me get your smokes, Dad," I whispered.

He didn't speak as I unlocked the door. I pushed Anna through and glared at Mom before giving Anna to her. I walked straight toward the front hall that led to the front door but stopped when I heard Dad yelling at Mom to come back with those no-good kids. Then I ran into Peter's room, where I knew I'd find a phone, and dialed 911.

A woman's voice asked me for my address.

"Twenty Wallace Street."

"What's the emergency, Ma'am?"

"Someone is going to get killed at my house if you don't send the police over right now," I said clearly into the receiver, and I realized for the first time that this was the fear that had been growing in me all day. Someone might get killed, someone I loved and cared about. Maybe me. Dad could kill us all if he wanted, and he might tonight.

Just then, I heard a loud crashing sound coming from the rear bedroom. I bolted down the front stairs with Anna right behind me. Peter, though three years older than me, couldn't escape, because after supper every night, he would go and sit on a portable commode. That night, he remained sitting, listening to everything and humming to himself as he created a giant yarn ball. How long had he been there? I was sure he wished that he could escape with us.

"I'll come back, Peter. Don't worry!" I yelled up the stairs.

Anna and I got down to the front porch, and we could hear Mom screaming. I pulled Anna's hand, and we headed toward the rear of the house and hid underneath the forsythia bushes.

"Where do you think Christina is?" I asked.

"Oh, she's probably playing with her dolls," Anna said with a smile, knowing Christina loved her dolls, especially when there was trouble.

"Does your head hurt?" I reached out and touched her temple. The blood on her hair and face was wet and sticky on my fingertips.

"Not as much as Dad's will when I bang him over the head with this!" She held up a red brick that a few days earlier we were using in our pretend game of "Free Patty Hearst."

"I never thought we'd get out of there." I looked up toward the house. "I hope Dad doesn't cover up all the blood. That's evidence to show the police."

The blue lights of the approaching police car flickered around and around as it drove down the street, searching for the correct house number. The sirens weren't on and I felt grateful. This was not the first time the police had come to our home. They should have known where we lived by then. Maybe they got so many calls from people on this street, it was hard to know which home to enter.

Anna and I watched from the side yard as two officers got out of the car. One of the officers carried a Billy club. I pictured it smashing down on Dad's head. I watched as they went through our front door, and I thought to myself how much more confident I'd be if I held a weapon in my hand, wore a badge, walked in heavy-soled shoes.

Anna and I heard men's voices coming out the kitchen windows. The police were talking to Dad. They sounded like they were having a regular old chat. Old friends hanging out after a long day's work. One of the officers came down the backstairs with a flashlight, looking for us. I came out first from our hiding place, and Anna was right behind me.

The man in blue said, "We're gonna let your Daddy stay under one condition. You children must mind him better. Do what he tells you the first time he tells you. Stop making trouble and he won't get so upset, 'cuz when he gets upset, he wants to drink, and drinking obviously doesn't make the problem any better. For him or you kids."

I shook my head like I was the horse with too many flies in my ears. "You don't understand. My dad gets this way no matter what we do."

The officer probably thought he was helping us with his expert advice, like he was Frank Poncherello from *Chips*. But I knew in that moment he had no clue what to do and would rather leave than force Dad to go. Maybe this cop had a dad like mine. Maybe he had children of his own whom he wished would mind him better.

"You have to make him go!" I said. "Look at what he did to my sister!" I pointed to my sister's bleeding head. "Did you look on the walls in the back bedroom?"

"Now young lady, it's that kind of attitude that got you and the rest of your family into this mess in the first place. Trust me. If you behave better, this sort of thing won't happen again." He walked toward the front of the house to meet his partner and averted his eyes from us. I knew if they left, Dad would consider this whole incident a victory.

I felt as enraged as a lion and helpless as a lamb. They should know better. They were supposed to protect us. They were the only ones Dad would obey, given that they had the law on their side. What did we have? We were just his little girls. Dad's property to do what he wanted with.

Anna and I went upstairs. Mom was helping Peter into his pajamas, and Christina was watching *Laverne and Shirley* as if nothing were wrong. I didn't see Dad and went with Anna into the kitchen, where he was sitting at the kitchen table and eating like he hadn't eaten in days.

When he finished, he said, "Clean up the mess you made."

1979

Rule of Law

Mom sat at the kitchen table, having coffee with Ronnie, a dark-haired Irish woman from Al-Anon. I stood behind my mother, my hands resting on her shoulders.

"It's time, Rose," Ronnie said softly. "You need to file a restraining order."

Mom stared into her empty coffee cup. "How will that help if he's still living with us?"

While Ronnie wasn't Mom's sponsor, she felt inclined to assist our family. Maybe our family reminded her of her own family. Maybe she recognized a part of herself in my mother. Maybe she was a kind person wanting to give back for all that she'd received. Anna and Christina were on the back porch, listening in through the screen door. We'd wait for Dad to leave for work before getting up ourselves and sometimes go to bed early, just so we wouldn't have to see him.

"A man can climb the highest mountain, but he can't dwell there long," Ronnie said. "A restraining order can be enough to keep some guys from doing anything again. That's been true with my second husband, Mickey, and me. After he beat me one time— one time—I filed, and we've been okay for a couple of years now; no more troubles, at least not physically. You've got to remember that guys respond to power moves."

"I can't see how it won't make him angrier."

"It probably will. But he can feel mad all he wants. He just can't hit you and the kids anymore and get away with it."

"It's that simple, huh? I just have to involve somebody bigger than me to get him to change? I never knew it would come to this." I heard the disappointment and resignation that would become so much a part of the story my mom would tell. Little did I know how far away she was from where she wanted to be, from where her own father would have wanted her to be, from where she deserved to be.

"Who are you kidding, Rose?" Ronnie smiled wryly, revealing not one, but two chipped teeth.

"Just myself, I guess." Mom put her head in her hands. "I feel so stupid. And ashamed."

"Women like us always feel stupid and ashamed. It's okay. Just don't let it stop you from doing what you know you need to do. For you and your kids."

A few days later, I overheard Mom on the phone, telling Ronnie that she'd gone to the police station.

"The cop told me I'm supposed to stay under the radar," she said. "As if that's possible. It's not easy to stay away from someone who lives with you, not to mention the problem of trying to live in a way that doesn't upset him. You know what I mean?"

It wasn't much, but at least she seemed to be trying.

Spring came around, offering occasional whiffs of the Atlantic Ocean and pussy willow blossoms. Dad's work slowed down, and he began coming home in the afternoons. Mom started taking us to the nearby park at Powderhouse Square as one way to keep the peace after school and before dinner. My sisters and I sat in our Catholic school uniforms, the knee socks held up with elastics so tight that they left deep grooves in the space behind our knees.

"Mom, can you help me with this one?" Anna pointed to a math problem. "I don't understand what I'm supposed to do."

"I'll help you, Anna. Here, give it to me," I said and reached for her notebook.

"No, I want Mommy to help me. She's better at math than you are, anyway."

I stuck my tongue out at her.

Christina had finished her work and laid her head on Mom's lap. Mom looked up into the sky. I imagined that she had flown to a place far from here, back to Sicily or California or Pennsylvania or maybe somewhere that I had traveled to only in my mind—a secluded island in the Pacific Ocean or a remote mountaintop in Africa where one can hear wild birds calling to one another in the darkness.

"We have to wait and hear if the women's shelter has housing for a family of five," Mom blurted out to no one. "I don't know what else to do."

She'd done it. It had taken her months after the night of the bloody wall, but she was finally protecting us. I watched maple seed blossoms float to the ground, descending from the limbs above our heads by the hundreds. Peter's kneecaps were covered in goose bumps, and I worried aloud that he might be cold.

"I fine, Rose-Marie." He pushed the sweatshirt away and clapped his hands together. He knew we were on the verge of something. It scared him a bit, but it also excited him.

"How come we have to leave our house, Mommy?" Christina asked.

"And why does *he* get to stay?" I didn't hide my sarcasm.

"While I try to get a restraining order against your dad, we have to put distance between him and us. It's the way it has to be right now."

It felt unfair—it felt massively unfair. But it was better than nothing.

Ronnie drove Mom, Anna, Christina, and me to the police station. Dad had come home late and drunk, and forced Mom into a corner in the pantry, cross-examining her before going to bed. We approached one of the officers, a different man from the one who had come to our house.

"Lady," he said, "you got to understand we're not social workers." He leaned back in his soft-cushioned swivel chair and raised his arms behind his head. "If you have to disagree less to make your days go smoother, then so be it."

Mom flinched as if she'd been slapped.

Ronnie banged her fist on the forest-green counter that jutted out in front of the glass separating the officer from her. "Where the hell is she supposed to go when she becomes afraid for her life? She's got four kids! It's her right to live in their house as much as his!"

"Let's just go," Mom said to Ronnie. "If he does anything again, we can come back, and they'll issue the order."

"Yeah, and when you're dead, a restraining order will come in really handy."

I walked ahead as we left the police station, making sure to step on the cracks in the pavement, remembering how I would try, as a child, to avoid landing on the fissures. That was a long time ago. I was fifteen. It felt strange to be in front of my mother, but more fitting, given how I hadn't experienced her guiding me for a long time. She wasn't taking care of us; she wasn't taking care of herself. She was staying with Dad for reasons I couldn't comprehend, and even if I knew what those reasons were, they wouldn't have mattered to me.

Sometimes when I was little, Mom and I would be together with no one else to interrupt us—not my sisters, not my brother, especially not Dad. I remember one afternoon, rare and precious, a balmy spring day where everything seemed possible for her, for me, for us. We weren't doing anything special, just running errands in Davis Square, and she'd watched me ride the horsie for a nickel outside Gorim's department store.

"Just press the gum against the back of your front teeth like this." She handed me a piece of gum when my ride ended. "And then blow very gently." I tried, and a large, translucent, bright-pink bubble appeared in front of my face. I grabbed Mom's hand with gusto.

"You did it, honey! See, I told you; all it takes is practice and you can do whatever you want."

After another afternoon sitting on the park bench, we came home from school to find Mom hunched over the bathroom sink with a wet washcloth over her right eye.

"What happened?" Anna asked.

"It's nothing. You kids go outside."

"We don't want to go outside." I said, "It's raining."

"Get outside!" She yelled, and her hand fell away from her face.

"We're not leaving," I said. "Where's Daddy?"

"He's trying to sleep."

"No, I'm not. There's too much racket in this goddamn house." Dad came into the small bathroom where Anna and I stood next to Mom. Christina was still helping Peter come up the front stairs, as it was her turn to get him in.

"Go to Ronnie's. Tell her I said it was okay." Mom said to me.

When Ronnie found out what had happened, she took my sister and me down to the police station, and Anna and I filed a complaint against Dad. Maybe something about two little girls showing up on their own to ask for help made it impossible to ignore.

The police then came to our home with the long-awaited restraining order in their hands. Dad tried to cajole them into thinking that nothing had happened, but Mom standing there with a shiner was hard to dismiss.

He tried another tack. "You know this is my house!"

"That's true, sir," one of the officers said, "and you'll have your say in court. But the law requires you to leave the premises."

"What sort of bullshit is this?" He gave them a long, cold stare, and I feared they would change their minds. The other officer told us kids to go and wait in the living room. Dad finally turned and went into his bedroom. They followed and watched him pack his bag. Nobody talked, and I wondered if the cops felt bad for him. Were they still on his side and just pretending? On the other hand, if they were finally helping us, did it really matter?

We had to go to court the next day. The judge asked all sorts of questions that made us feel naked to the world. I felt like I was going to throw up the whole time.

"How often are you afraid of your dad hurting you or your mother?" The judge looked over her glasses and down at us from her seat behind the podium. She tried to be nice while we talked about "not very nice" things.

"Well, all the time," Anna said, then paused. "I mean, not all."

The rest of us looked at her like she was crazy. I said quickly, "What she means is that she's not afraid all the time. That's 'cuz she's tough. But my dad tries to make us afraid every chance he gets."

The quiet in the room covered us like one of Nana's crocheted blankets. Mom was crying, but I felt no sympathy for her. It was her fault we were in this mess.

Dad had been summoned as well, but he didn't come. I wasn't that surprised; he thought he was above the law most of the time.

As she continued her questioning, I sensed strongly that the judge truly wanted to help us. "What happens when he drinks? Does he ever hit you when he's not drunk? Has he ever been drunk in public? What happens then?" She read her questions as if from a list but listened intently to the answers. I tried to keep a poker face. If I let anyone know how I felt, it might jinx the whole thing.

The judge ordered a recess, and my sisters and I all went to the bathroom. Cousin Bette had stayed out in the waiting room with my brother during proceedings, and Mom now went and sat with them. While we were in the bathroom, we play-acted this scene: "And how long has your father beaten you, little lady?" Anna climbed up on the sink and looked the part, trying not to giggle.

Christina stood next to her. She liked the large, chrome-framed mirror and got so close she almost went cross-eyed. "Oh, since I was very young, your highness. Oops, I mean your honor."

I added in a voice made to sound younger, "I remember being a baby. And I'm in the crib and my daddy chased my mommy round and round with a butcher knife." I looked up, and we laughed in unison, our mouths open wide and our heads thrown back.

A toilet flushed and out of the stall walked the judge. She looked at all of us and said, "You never know who might be listening, girls." She washed her hands slowly and reached out to stroke Christina's cheek. Christina stared up in adoration and almost left with her.

"Come back here, Christina. You're not with her. You're with us!" Anna took her hand.

"I want to be a judge when I grow up." Christina said, "I want to tell everybody that they have to be nice to one another. Daddy, too!"

"You can't ever tell Daddy what to do," I said and waved at them to leave the bathroom.

The judge made a motion to suspend a ruling because of my dad's absence. She withheld the restraining order for another week, meaning not only that we had to come back, but also that Dad could stay. I hated the judge more than I'd ever hated anyone, even my parents. She could have done something and didn't!

All hell broke loose that weekend, starting with Dad making us clean house and do yard work all day. The only thing that made it bearable was my blasting the hi-fi, something that made Mom edgy, but which Dad never seemed to mind. While I washed the kitchen floor, enjoying the way Scruffy chased the mop like it was alive, I sang along to the lyrics of the latest Queen hit, "We Are the Champions," knowing full well that like a lot of teen age girls, I'd had my share of sand kicked in my face.

Fortunate Daughter

Dad went to a union meeting, which gave us a little break, but he returned home plastered at around three o'clock that afternoon. At first, he went up to the attic to howl for an hour. Then he came down into the kitchen, looking for a fight.

Why he thought picking on people smaller and weaker than him made him bigger, I didn't understand. It wasn't like we didn't know he was the man of the house. Even without the violence, he was one of the most indomitable people I knew. I remembered standing on the street, days after the blizzard of '78 had started, and hearing all our neighbors cheer because Dad came back home after a full day of delivering groceries to the supermarkets of New England, despite nearly one hundred deaths on local roads.

No one was cheering for him today. Mom was ready for him and had our bags in the car. I had been writing a letter to President Carter at my desk but came downstairs when he did.

"Go outside with your brother and sisters," she said to me. Her voice sounded icy.

He grabbed her by the elbow. "What makes you think you have any say here?"

"We'll leave, Ned. It's clear you don't want to be around us."

"Don't tell me what I want!" He shoved her into a corner of the kitchen and poked her in the chest hard with his finger, the way I'd seen him do as far back as I could recall.

"Mom."

Both my parents looked at me like they didn't know any of us were still there. She'd been threatening to leave for a long time. This time I wanted to make sure she did it.

"Just go, Rose-Marie. I'll be down in a minute." She said this like she was in the middle of looking for her purse. Just another day. Just another outing.

I turned and held Christina's small hand in my own. Anna was already helping Peter down the stairs when we heard Mom scream, following what sounded like a wallop to her belly.

"How does it feel to be the big boss now?" Dad said loud enough for us to hear. "If you want to run things, you've got to take the consequences."

We hurried outside and waited in the car. Somehow Mom got away, and she came running out of the house about ten minutes later—though not before Anna stuck her finger in the cigarette lighter. I told her not to do it, but she did it anyway. And now she was crying. As if we didn't have enough to cry about.

This time we went straight to RESPOND, a brand-new battered women's shelter and one of the first in the country. Two women greeted Mom at the address Ronnie had given her. We didn't even get out of the car. We followed behind as the two staff drove us to a secret asylum.

It was a ten-story high-rise made of beige, pockmarked concrete in a housing development filled with broken windows and slender, dark pipes used as railings both inside and outside of the apartments. Poor white families, mostly single-mother households with children of all ages, filled the place—sitting on stairwells, hanging out windows, running barefoot over glass-strewn tar. Older kids with dirty faces and hair sticking straight up ran to sit on the pavement as we pulled up. As we quietly unloaded our car, they watched us without shame like we were the newest TV show, murmuring to one another, covering their mouths and giggling. I could feel my heart pounding in my chest.

Did they know we'd gone into hiding? That RESPOND was housing us? Or were the circumstances of their lives such that our few belongings and sad affect were not out of the ordinary?

"Can I go play, Mommy?" Christina asked immediately.

"Not yet, Christina-Lou." I tried to speak casually, as if we'd just arrived at a vacation resort, and we were going to eat before going for a swim. "We have to help Mommy unpack and make supper together."

Christina asked Mom again, this time more insistently. I grabbed her arm a little too tightly as Anna attempted to help Peter inside. "Handicapped Accessible" didn't exist back then.

"Ouch, you're hurting me. Mom, Rose-Marie just hurt me."

"That's enough, girls. Rose-Marie, let her go. I'm the mother here."

"Yeah, right. And doing a great job."

My words hung in the sour-smelling air of the hallway outside our temporary apartment. I didn't feel sorry for what I'd said, even though I knew it hurt her.

"Christina," she said finally, "go help Anna get Peter up these stairs, and Rose-Marie, take in the bags." It was as if I'd never spoken.

We lived there for nearly two weeks. It was not at all like being on vacation. Nothing worked right, and everything stank of mold or pee. The kids were tough in a way that caused us to feel constantly afraid anytime we left our two-bedroom, half-a-bathroom, no-living-room apartment.

"You think you better than us," a girl who'd been eyeing me from below a streetlight said. She was a bit shorter than me but a whole lot rounder, and her forehead was wider than it should've been.

I'd just drawn a four-square court on the tar with a piece of broken chalk I'd hit upon. Christina was with me. After the girl had thrown out her challenge, she sauntered over to me. Some kids seemed to appear out of nowhere all around her, her challenge to me the bugle call of their assemblage.

"No, I don't," I said in an even voice, and I meant it. I didn't understand people acting like they were better than someone else. I'd had too many experiences of witnessing Peter being gawked at to buy into that one, and my Catholic education pounded in the value of humility every chance it could.

She pointed to the square. "Then why think you can decide what games we gonna play?"

"You don't have to play." I put my arm around Christina. I wished Liana, my friend from the neighborhood, was here. Though younger than me, she'd tell them all to fuck off and enjoy watching them back down. Anna, too, would have prized the opportunity to shove this girl out of our way.

"We want to play," a child that looked like a younger sibling said. I couldn't tell if it was a boy or girl and it distracted me for a minute.

"Only if I'm captain," the girl said, and I could tell if I didn't agree quickly, even though this game had no captains, I'd be in trouble.

"Okay," I said coolly. "You got a ball?"

Back at home, outside was the place we were most safe. Here, it was the opposite. So, we watched a lot of TV. *Mork and Mindy* made us laugh, and *Dallas* made us believe that our crisis was nothing compared to the outrageous cruelty of the filthy rich. We couldn't eat our regular meals because the stove was tiny and there weren't enough pans. Mom responded with "Beggars can't be choosers" anytime she overheard one of us complaining.

She drove us to school and picked us up in between getting Dad to move out. With the law more on our side than before, she felt more at ease packing up his stuff and talking with him about the logistical fallout of his departure. We didn't hear from our relatives, even though they must have known something was up. Maybe Mom wouldn't go to them for fear they'd say, "I told you so."

Ella and Dr. Yaffe came by to check up on us—not to have therapy talks, but to make out whether everything was okay and make sure that we were adjusting all right.

Fortunate Daughter

When we returned home two weeks later, our house seemed huge, partly because Dad's absence showed how much space he'd taken up and because we'd just experienced a life that truly was more cramped and grueling. I lay belly-down on my bed and drank in the smell of cleanliness. I sat at my desk—the one I had painted myself—and touched my papers like old friends. I opened the drawers of my bureau top to bottom just to see my clothes, and I felt lucky. Lucky as a dime!

My siblings and I thought Dad might really be gone for good and were trying to decide what that meant. He'd left without saying goodbye and without giving us any idea as to when we would see him again. I was surprised that his departure didn't feel as good as I'd expected. Anna, Christina, Peter, and I wondered where he'd gone. Mom didn't know. Before a week was out, we were asking, what did we do wrong? Could we have loved him more? Could we have been more lovable? And if so, wouldn't everything have been okay?

1980

Overthrow

Mom brought my sisters and me to visit Dad. I imagine that she must have felt conflicted about arranging such a visit and scared for our family's well-being. Dad had been out of the house for a few months, and one of my uncles found out that he'd been renting a room at a boarding house in Lowell. I knew that we all missed him, that I missed him and that it didn't make sense. She stayed in the car while my sisters and I entered the dark interior of Malone's, a local bar. Three young girls standing in the smoky doorway was enough for the room to become silent in the heavy darkness.

The bartender asked, "Can I help you ladies?"

Dad, who'd been sitting at the bar, turned his head slowly. He got off his stool and walked toward us with an awkward expression. He looked older than I remembered him, and skinnier.

"You girls gonna just stand there like cows waiting to get milked?" He motioned to a round table that had four empty chairs.

We slid into our seats and talked with him for about an hour. It wasn't hard. We felt relief in just knowing he was alive but tried hard not to show any feelings. It felt easy to be with him.

If we gave Mom the thumbs-up, then she would invite him to return home. This responsibility burdened me, but I couldn't articulate it, even with Ella. In some ways, I appreciated the control Mom was giving us, but I also felt my resentment building. Her inability to be the adult I wanted her to be, needed her to be, made me so angry at her.

After our visit, Mom went and saw him by herself. A week later, he came back home. To live with us and try again.

My parents sold the two-family at No. 20, and we moved up the street to a single-family home. It needed a lot of repair, but it was at street level, which made it easier for Peter to maneuver in and out on his own. It also had a bathroom on the first floor, which also gave him more freedom.

While Dad had ceased overtly sexually abusing me, he remained an unsavory force in all our lives—staring inappropriately at our developing breasts, telling dirty jokes, sharing information with us that Mom had told him in private.

I grew increasingly grateful for Ella and Dr. Yaffe. They were seeing my whole family, even Dad, at this point, and it seemed no small coincidence that their presence in our lives was in direct proportion to Dad's change for the better. Be that as it may, I stayed vigilant around him, even when we watched the Steelers defeat the Cowboys 35–31 in Super Bowl XIII.

I pointed to Terry Bradshaw and asked, "How does someone so small not get hurt more often playing with such big guys?"

Daddy pointed to the defensive line. "It's the job of those other big guys to protect him."

"What if they mess up?"

"It's possible, but not likely in this game."

Dad tried hard to remain sober, but rather than seek out support from a therapist or truly become a member of AA, he went at it solo. Ironically, this contributed to making him more irritable and easier to upset. Because he was no longer drinking, none of us felt like we had the right to complain or challenge him when he treated us badly.

I particularly disliked how he took up so much space around

the house. He was around more, especially on the weekends, crankier than ever, and demanding we stay busy doing chores almost nonstop.

"You'll finish eating those green beans if it takes you all night," he would yell at Christina.

"Is that where you put up the gardening tools?" he would yell at me, and then make me clean out the whole shed from top to bottom.

"Not a Phillips-head, a flat-head screwdriver! How many times have I told you?" He would scold my brother, who didn't understand, no matter how harsh Dad became.

Mom tried hard to make everything just right to show her support for his sobriety. My younger sister, Christina, also got more hopeful. She'd tell stories at the supper table about kids growing up in happy families who went away to camp over the summer or invited their whole class over for huge sleepover parties. I think they were meant to inspire us. Peter, too, would do his best to provide camaraderie for Dad by offering to help him wash and wax the car. They'd also sit together and watch *The Dukes of Hazard*, all the while jesting with one another about jacked up cars, busty girls, or both.

Because we were now all teenagers, we were also more independent. Christina and I began attending Alateen meetings in South Boston. The South Boston-Dorchester area was still recovering from the busing movement and almost entirely white Irish Catholic. We'd walked past a plethora of bar rooms, not unlike those in our home town: wiry children going someplace fast, with or without an adult to hold their hands, the smell of the ocean at Castle Island, radios blasting out at full volume the coverage of the IRA's unsuccessful attempt to assassinate Margaret Thatcher. Not only did going to meetings get us out of the house, we were able to hang out with other young people like ourselves, struggling to overcome domestic injustice.

"I can't do it anymore," Johnny, one of the meeting regulars, said. "The next time he mouths off to my mother, I'm going to haul off and kill him."

"Don't go thatching your roof on a windy day, Johnny," another regular, Cindy, told him and placed her hand on his knee. She was tiny, but at almost twenty-one, she was an elder in our group.

"He has no right to say what he says about her, she's my mum, for Christ's sake!" Johnny shook his head and searched for a place to put out his cigarette. I passed the ashtray over. His words resonated.

"I'm not saying there isn't a time and a place to say something," another member said. I hadn't seen him before, but he looked like he was from Southie. His white sneakers almost shone, they were so clean. "A wise head keeps his mouth shut sometimes." A lot of nods. "We have to be a bit willing to recognize that what we want to do and what's good for us to do aren't always the same thing."

Most, if not all, of these kids were uncompromising in their identity as Irish Catholics and what they believed, but they were warm toward us in a way that felt sincere. The Alateen meeting acted as an equalizer, and kids, myself included, felt safe to cry or yell about a brother who'd just overdosed or an uncle who just died of liver failure or a mom who'd gone missing weeks prior. Southie kids were wildly complex in their ability to accept you, defend you, understand you, but also act like relationships only mattered in the here and now. Who knew anything about tomorrow? Who would be alive, even?

When I read over my journal entries one day, I realize how depressed and embittered I had become.

Mom is such an idiot! She keeps thinking that if she does what Dad tells her, it will make him happy. Is she out of her fuck'n mind? And she's always quick to tell me how like him I am. Am I supposed to feel complimented? She only says it when I'm doing something she can't stand, which is most of the time these days. I can't stand living in this crazy house. I wish Anna, Christina, and Peter and I could live in our own place and Mom and Dad could have each other to themselves!

One evening, Dad brought me to a talk given by an Armenian photographer named Aram Narsesian. This man had recently returned from a tour of Vietnam, Thailand, and Laos and was showing slides of those persecuted by the Pol Pot regime. He likened the massacre of the 1.5 million Cambodian people to the Armenian genocide, which had affected him personally. I'd just finished reading the *Diary of Anne Frank* and couldn't believe that the world had allowed another massacre of this magnitude to occur.

"Our government knew those people were dying and didn't do anything to stop them?" I asked Dad.

"Government action never fully reflects the will of the people, not here or elsewhere in the world."

"All those skulls piled up. They were real people?"

"Every last one of them."

Dad was an active union member and, in many respects, a socialist in his viewpoint. He seemed to know a lot about world politics. Now that he was staying sober, I was seeing just how much I'd been influenced by him in this regard, although it infuriated me that he could be so knowledgeable about suffering in the larger world, and yet the cause so much of it. These contradictions gave my cynicism a lot to work with. Another diary entry:

He thinks just because he takes me to hear a lecture or see a movie, I'm his friend? Is he out of his fucking mind? It doesn't matter to me that the things he lets me do are interesting or cool. That's always been his trick to getting me. But I don't believe that he does anything for me. Everything he's ever done is for him. Just because he didn't do what he wanted to do with his life and just because he blames everyone else for his failures doesn't mean I believe him, not for one minute! The two of them can have one another! I bet he starts drinking again next week when he realizes his plan of winning me over didn't work! Why did he have to come home? I didn't want him to die alone out there, but why did she let him back again?

One morning, I noticed the smell of Saturday morning leftovers as I came up from the basement, my arms heavy with a basket of still-warm laundry. Fried potatoes, Spam, and toasted Italian bread will forever mean Dad's cooking.

I was sixteen and mulling over John Lennon's assassination. Why would anyone want to kill someone who could see so much about what was wrong with the world, and more importantly, what did we need to do to make it right? It was comforting to know that every person who knew of his death was in full agreement about its tragedy. Dad sat by the glass doors leading out to the back porch wearing a large, corduroy one-piece, a navy blue scally cap, and steel-toed work boots. The same boots I probably learned how to tie when I was a little girl.

"Where's your mother?" he asked me sharply, without looking up.

"I dunno. Maybe she's taking a shower," I answered, and kept walking.

"I thought she would've cleaned herself up hours ago," he muttered.

I didn't take the bait and kept walking into Peter's room toward the bathroom. I could hear the TV on in the living room. Peter was watching *The Incredible Hulk*, who had to let the world go on thinking that he was dead, until he could find a way to control the raging spirit that dwelt within him. I could hear my sisters upstairs in their bedroom, giggling, wrestling, cleaning up. I needed to keep track, because Dad often tried to provoke one of us into having a fight with him by asking us to defend the actions of another. I put the basket of laundry down outside the bathroom door and knocked softly so Dad couldn't hear me: I wanted to warn Mom that he was looking for a fight.

I heard Mom unravel a towel off the hook that hung near the window before she opened the bathroom door slowly. "I'll be out in a minute."

I smelled lavender talcum powder—an odor that had come to mean Mom to all of us. She poked her head out while her hair was still wet; it framed her face such that she looked even smaller than usual and somehow older. Had she always been such a tiny person? Or was it that I had grown so much larger than her, with big breasts and wider hips? On my birthday, she'd laughed about how someone my size could have ever come out of her.

"Dad's looking for a fight, Mom," I told her, and turned to walk up the stairs that led up to my sisters' room on the third floor.

I smiled at the sound of my sisters as they lumbered down the stairs leading from the second floor to the first, enjoying the knowledge that their noise would anger Dad. And how they would be surprised, once again, by how easy it was to upset him. Such stupidity! Not to mention Mom's idiocy in working her hardest to kowtow to his demands, even though it made no difference, either.

Suddenly, Scruffy yelped, and I felt everyone in the house freeze.

"God-damn dog!" Dad yelled. "Always getting under my feet. Rose-Marie, I thought I made it clear I never wanted a dog in the house!"

Scruffy had been our dog for six years by then, and Dad made it sound like we had just picked him up yesterday.

My sisters and I moved toward the kitchen doorway. I placed my hand on Mom's shoulder before I even realized that she was standing there. She usually wanted to be the first one to enter a room when Dad got violent. Lamb to the slaughter!

Scruffy was lying against the far corner of the kitchen. His tiny body was trembling with his head low to the floor, but I heard him growl. He was aware that he shouldn't push it, but Scruffy had his pride.

"Ned!" Mom shouted and then quickly lowered her voice. "I'll put him back outside if that's what you want. He must have come in with you." She went to grab Scruffy by the collar.

Before she reached him, Dad pulled back her arm and slapped her full in the face. She landed hard in one of the chairs that surrounded the table.

Not one of us spoke; we just moved. Anna jumped on Dad's back, and Christina grabbed hold of one of his arms. At forty-one years old, he stood six feet, two inches and weighed a good 210 pounds. He'd been a truck driver nearly his entire adult life, and the muscles in his arms and legs were big and hard from all the lifting. We didn't care.

They caught him by surprise and brought him down. Once he was down with his back against the floor, I sprang onto his chest and began punching him repeatedly as hard as I could. On his face and shoulders and neck. Over and over again.

It was the first time in my life I'd ever done anything like that. It felt both right and long overdue.

Lying on his back, with my knee on his chest, he did all he could to protect his face by raising his forearms in the shape of a wishbone.

I thought, *Wish you weren't getting beat on, Daddy? Wish you had daughters who knew how to behave better? Daughters who respected you enough to never attack you? Never go at you three on one? Wish your life were different every day you opened your eyes?*

Anna was punching him, too. She slammed him in the belly as he tried to bend his legs to protect himself. Mom hadn't stopped screaming but was also not doing a thing to get us off him. She hadn't even started her usual routine of running around to lower the blinds and checking to make sure that all the storms were down so the neighbors wouldn't hear. That was usually what she did when she knew there was going to be "a scene."

Even Scruffy got in on the action and bit Dad's shoes and the bottom of his pant legs. That is when I looked up and saw a flash of metal.

Christina was waving a knife—our big carving knife—over Dad's head. She was still in her flannel nightgown with the ruffled cotton collar and red star buttons.

"Get out of the way! Let me finish this!" she yelled.

Anna and I quickly rolled off Dad, leaving him on the floor, breathing deeply, holding his gut.

"Christina, put that down!" Mom, looking a lot like the Mary in the bathtub statue in the backyard, moved toward my sister with her arms open, palms face up.

"Don't come near me or I'll kill him," I heard Christina whisper.

It didn't cross my mind to stop her. I had spent many a day expecting to discover the death of various family members. I would often imagine everyone in pools of blood after having their heads shot off. Other times, I would see them lying peacefully in their own beds after being poisoned. Ella had told me that these fantasies might be wishful thinking.

Anna said, "Christina, you don't need to kill him. He's learned his lesson." Dad was still on the floor, but he crawled to the side of the room with his back against the wall. He looked a shade whiter than usual.

"I don't care. I want this all to end. I don't want him to keep making it so we can never have any peace."

My baby sister. She sounded so grown-up when she said this. I reached for the hand that wasn't holding the knife. Her fingers were cold and listless, like she was dead.

Mom cried quietly and stood now with her arms around my brother's shoulders. He had rolled himself into the room.

Fortunate Daughter

"You don't want to do something that'll make your life more miserable, Christina," I said.

She lowered her arm and bowed her head. Anna came over and stood on the other side of her, and she dropped the knife to the floor. As a threesome, we left the room and went upstairs. That moment passed, followed by other moments far less tense or encouraging. But that didn't matter. What mattered was that moment existed. For my sisters and I to find ourselves present in the story as something bigger than meek and compliant was a universe away from being absent from it, being written out of it altogether. Physically attacking our dad became the toehold on the wall leading up and out, into a future free of fear.

Dad must have risen from the floor and gone out the back door. I didn't hear him leave, but it made sense to me that he wouldn't want to stick around. Then I overheard Peter ask Mom, "Can I watch *Scooby Doo*, Mommy?" and I felt the tiniest bit of hope. We'd taken him on, and we'd won. For the first time, we'd won.

Moonlit Walk

t sixteen years old, I spent nearly the whole summer living with Gramma, my dad's mother. At prayer meeting one night, I led the small church group in their biweekly discourse about Genesis 39 NIV. I didn't know what they expected of me, a person both inside and outside their group, but I did know that the conversation, as steered by me that evening in my unfamiliar role as Bible teacher, went in a direction many of them, including me, had not anticipated. The room, stuffy and thick with perspiration, held us in our search for meaning.

"I agree with you that the story of Potiphar's wife is a good example of a woman being deceitful and . . . " I didn't know what word to use. Should I choose "unreliable" or, better yet, "dishonest"? I decided and said, "Untrustworthy." The group, about twenty or so, more than half of them women, and most of them over fifty, stared back at me. I was expected to go on, so I did. "But in other parts of the Bible, you can find a different take on that same quality of falsehood."

Everyone, including Gramma, looked at me like I'd just spoken in tongues. We remained secrets from one another, and I from myself.

"Where would you find *yourself* one of those so-called passages?" asked Harold, an old-timer who appeared typecast in the role of Southern bigot, both in his dress and expression of ideas. I knew that he'd decided the minute he realized who would be teacher that night what his role would be. He loved to reference the Bible as a matter of fact, anytime he stated anything, especially something racist, daring anyone listening to question not just him, but God's intentions on the issue at hand. Most no one ever did.

"Exodus 2, for instance," I said. "Doesn't Moses' mother circumvent the pharaoh's order to kill all of the baby boys and save her son? Isn't that manipulative but at the same time essential to her survival, for our survival?"

"I reckon she's got a point," said Linzey, one of my father's brothers and a deacon at Hall's Chapel, once again revealing himself as a man ahead of his time.

Things had settled down back at home in Somerville. The physical attack on Dad had made an impact on all our interactions that years of AA, therapy, and hopefulness never had. Perhaps it was because Dad finally knew that if he tried anything else, one of us would kill him in his sleep.

Ironically, this face-off had created a shift that pierced my heart like a sharp blade. I remained an A student, but I felt more isolated from my peer group and increasingly self-conscious about my appearance, my thoughts, and my place in this world.

Things grew quieter, and I'd found myself becoming more curious about Dad as a person. How did he come to be the man he was—husband, father, truck-driver, philosopher? A part of me, that I don't think I could have named, realized that the trail to his identity led back to his hometown, Buckskin, North Carolina, the place he'd been born and raised and where I'd lived as a child for a few years.

Although it was 1980, Dad's side of the family were a people who spoke a different tongue, wore different clothes, laughed at different jokes, and even honored a different God than I'd been raised to believe in. But they were family, and in the way that blood unites us, I felt compelled to find out what I didn't know about Dad, who he was and who he'd become—and, in turn, why I was. No him; no me.

Of course, the fantasy I had of spending time with family in a more rural setting didn't calculate the costs of what living with Gramma would truly feel like, nor how my absence from home would affect Mom and my siblings. Two months at Grandma's, gathering thin-shelled eggs from the chicken house, picking small, crimson strawberries in snake-filled fields, meandering with my cousins through unkempt forests, hanging wet laundry in the sun, eating tough-to-chew bear meat, shooting a .22 at plastic jugs, and swimming in the rushing river.

"Are you coming down?" I asked Dad, trying hard to feign indifference as I stood in the small entryway at the back of Gramma's house, the second week of August, near the anticipated end of my visit.

"It depends," he said.

"On what?" I asked, still trying to sound like it didn't matter to me.

"On you."

"You don't care one way or the other?"

"Not exactly. I'm thinking you may not want me to be there."

That I hadn't expected. "It's fine with me," I told him, and was surprised to find that it was. I'd stopped feeling afraid—really afraid—a while ago, and I was curious to see what he'd be like "back home," as he liked to call it.

"All right then, I'll leave tomorrow."

I felt my heart race and the sound of Gramma's singing in the background annoyed me. She had an uncanny way of appearing engrossed in one thing to mask her nosy interest in another. In this case, the smell of berries, sugar, and lard made up for it, and I couldn't begrudge her wanting to know if her oldest son was going to visit.

"You'll be getting in late, then," I said, and scraped the inside of my wrist where some poison ivy had turned up, despite the "alcohol rubdown." Most of my younger cousins spent all summer enveloped in large patches of bleeding red, all over their bodies, neck, belly, and between their fingers, even. They seemed unbothered, but I hated how it felt and couldn't keep myself from scratching.

"No, I'll sleep all morning and leave in the middle of the day and get there close to sunrise. It's always better that way."

"I'm sure Gramma will have breakfast ready, no matter what time you get in. Isn't that right, Gramma?"

Gramma, pretending not to eavesdrop, moved about the house, agitated like a swallow heading north.

I hung up the heavy black phone and rubbed my hands on my jeans, still dirty from berry picking before the sun rose. It had been hot, and I got stung a couple of times. Big bumble bees and yellow jackets swarmed everywhere. But the cobbler Gramma was currently cooking in the kitchen made up for a lot.

"What your dad say?" she asked me, a little too eagerly. "Is she gonna let him go?"

"I don't think it's got much to do with my mom."

Gramma rolled the extra dough into biscuits. "'To the woman the Lord said, "Your desire will be for your husband, and he will rule over you."' Genesis. 2:18; 3:16. She never lets him do anything without having something to say about it. It's not really a woman's place to tell her husband what to do. That's part of the reason he's been so miserable up North. Oh, Lord have mercy, I can't believe how long he's stayed up there."

I'd grown used to this kind of talk. Gramma didn't care one bit that she was speaking this way about my mother, her own daughter-in-law. Of course, she talked mean about everybody, but mostly every woman; none of her children's wives did anything right. And she always threw in some Biblical reference to back her up. She kept her King James right by the kitchen table and read it every day, relentlessly, looking for passages that backed up her judgments.

"1 Corinthians 11: 'Now I want you to realize that the head of every man is Christ, and the head of the woman is man, and the head of Christ is God.'" Thus, ended the lesson.

Despite her endless and harsh pronouncements, I loved being there. Everyone in Dad's family was curious about our lives up North, and they welcomed me, including me as if I'd always been there. Linzey included me on his milk runs, and Stanley went out of the way to involve me in gun practice with his son. I wondered if they understood the things I knew about Dad, and if they did, how come nobody brought it up with me? Standing next to my uncles was similar enough to standing near Dad that I would at times feel his presence, strong yet nonthreatening. Were they acting kindly to make up for Dad's sins?

Not since we left North Carolina and moved back to Massachusetts in the spring of 1970 had any of us—except for Dad—visited, not even when Grampa died. Dad made his annual trek down every summer, but Mom adamantly refused to join him or permit him to take any of us. Mom's stance was difficult for me to comprehend and appreciate as a child, especially since I had such fond memories of North Carolina.

"Why don't you young'uns get us some fresh eggs from the henhouse?"

Gramma was at the stove making biscuits out of Crisco and white flour. Out in the yard, dozens of blond chicks ran around various mommy hens. Our overpowering desire to catch one, and the fun of it, quickly distracted us from the task at hand.

While living in Morganton, we often went to see Dad's family, since they lived only little ways away, up in the Blue Ridge Mountains. Whatever the season, whatever problems Mom may have had feeling accepted by the McMahans or loved by Dad, my siblings and I loved going there. In the spring, my sisters and I would get up early to the sound of the rooster's crowing outside the kitchen window, the wet grass sparsely covered with dew-soaked spider webs that looked like large, outstretched snowflakes. Everyone else was still asleep, except Gramma.

In the late summer, the grandkids would sneak out to the cornfield on the south-facing hillside and eat raw corn off the stalk. We saved the shuck and silk for the milk cows that gazed at us, poking their heads through the wooden fence and reaching for us with their long, rasping tongues.

"Go on, Christina, you won't get bit. They don't really have teeth." I showed how much I trusted the cows by letting one of them lick my armpit. We giggled, picked corn out of our teeth, and shooed flies away from their eyelashes and the tops of our heads.

In the fall, we'd often gather sweet Limber twig apples that fell to the ground and attracted honeybees.

"Why are you crying, Rose-Marie?" Daddy asked me once. He sat under an old ash tree with a big knife he was using to cut an apple into pieces.

"I don't know. My foot hurts, a lot."

He looked at my foot. "Well, we got us a bee sting," he said, and my cousins gathered around. "Good for the joints. Come on over here, Jake," Daddy said to one of my uncles. "Bring that blanket. I know the perfect remedy for bee stings in little feet like yours."

I hopped onto the blanket, and everyone who could threw me in the air to divert my attention from the fiery sensation that lingered.

I'd forget how sad or mad I felt in these random, joyful moments. I was five years old and believed we were all going to be okay, that Mommy would spend more time with us, that Daddy wouldn't be mean, that my sisters and brother and I would be able to someday go to Disneyland.

Moonlit Walk

Sometimes Anna, Christina, and I would join Uncle John, another one of my father's six siblings, while he milked the cows. He laughed and squirted milk into our small mouths as he pulled on the cow's teat, filling the bucket at his feet.

Grampa, who loved to hunt, would often include as many grandchildren as wanted to go on squirrel-hunting adventures in the winter. We'd trudge behind him in the deep, white snow, doing our best to be quiet as we watched our warm breath evaporate in the cold air.

Visiting my grandparents in the mountains was idyllic compared to what went on at home. But now that I was growing up, I could understand why Mom might want to keep her distance from Gramma's tongue.

Dad was born and raised in western North Carolina in the mid-twentieth century agrarian communities, cut off by mountain ranges, Baptist congregations. Small cloistered towns where people were forced out of their sinful ways by social condemnation and religious declarations that were difficult, if not impossible, to dispute.

Why, if he loved it so much, did he leave at such a young age and join the Navy? That morning on the phone, in addition to sounding deferential, I got the sense he was flattered that my journey to adulthood and self-discovery included a trip back to North Carolina, his home. Perhaps he didn't know that I was standing up to his family much the same way I'd learned to stand up to him. The opportunity to be alone in the natural world and the distance from Mom and my siblings gave me perspective on my role in our family, something Ella had been trying to get me to consider more deeply of late.

The night before Dad arrived, Gramma stewed deer meat with gravy and biscuits, steamed corn on the cob, and sliced large beef-steak tomatoes with a few raw pieces of sweet white onion, which grew in her garden. As I finished my remaining bite of fresh blackberry cobbler for dessert, I knew that I was enjoying one of the last mountain meals of my visit.

After we cleaned up the dishes, we sat on the back porch. As was their custom, a few of my uncles and cousins stopped by. Gramma sat on the back steps that led out of her kitchen onto the porch and rested her hand on a good walking stick.

"So, Rose-Marie got a lift from an old mountain man today, did she?" Uncle Stanley asked, spitting tobacco juice out the side of his mouth. I told him about getting lost in the laurel during a walk I had taken that afternoon.

"Even the dogs was no good in helping her find her way back," said Josh, with a wry smile on his face. He was Lewis' second child and only boy. He was only ten years old and had wandered with me through these woods many an afternoon during my stay that summer.

"Nor shooting that .22 in the air," said Uncle Linzey, looking at Gramma. She had told him that when I hadn't returned in a reasonable time, she had gone in the backyard and shot toward the sky, hoping I'd hear it and find my way back.

Uncle Lewis, a Free Will Baptist minister, went for scripture, as he so often did in conversation. "'How often I have longed to gather your children together, as a hen gathers her chicks under her wings.' Luke 13:34."

Gramma chimed in. "'From infancy, you have known the Holy Scriptures, which is able to make you wise for salvation through faith in Christ Jesus. All scripture is God-breathed and is useful for teaching, rebuking, correcting, and training in righteousness.' Second Timothy."

After that, the conversation deteriorated into dueling scriptures. I tried to insert myself: "I think I might have been okay if I could've followed those dogs. But the laurel bushes were too thick, and they crawled into places that I just . . ."

"'I have gone astray like a lost sheep; seek thy servant; for I do not forget thy commandments.' Psalms 119:176."

Then, out of the blue, Gramma asked, "Do any of you young'uns want to go lookin' for four-leaf clovers?"

About six of the children under the age of seven jumped up to go with her. She was notorious for finding their delicate and unforeseen petals amid the grass. Uncle Linzey said, "It's fine just watching the sun set on Chestnut Mountain."

I felt the most at ease with Uncle Linzey, the family progressive, and that evening he talked about getting ready to go searching for methylate and witch hazel in the fall. He and some of my other uncles often located these plants and made what they termed "good money" from local herbalists who paid them for finding such things.

Linzey was tall and stoop-shouldered like Dad, but there was nothing in his presence that hinted at offhand violence. He was soft-spoken when he read scripture at Hall's Chapel, the Baptist Church that the McMahans had been attending for years, and his own children ran around like wild things with no fear. To be sure, when the family assembled themselves at post-church barbeques, one of his other brothers often remarked that he should give his two boys a good whooping now and again to keep them in line. But his gentle response was always, "I ain't gonna hurt my young'uns the same way Daddy done to us."

I wondered that summer how Linzey was so clear about something I don't think my own dad believed or could begin to act on. From what I could discover, whatever Dad said about cherishing his childhood, he could barely wait to leave home. I began then to wonder if it was more than Grampa's harsh words and sudden temper that motivated him to join the Navy when he was sixteen years old. Why wouldn't his other siblings have chosen the same path? Did something worse happen to him than what happened to them? Had he been molested and never told anyone, or worse, told someone and not been believed? Could a boy—the oldest son, no less—of his generation have told someone that sort of thing and been rescued?

He married my mother and had children whom he treated horribly a lot of the time, knowing all too well the harm that resulted. How come he turned out more like Grampa than his brothers who had stayed? Why had he allowed himself to be so brutal?

The next morning, Dad arrived at six o'clock exactly. I can still see the tangerine-colored Bronco coming up the gravel-strewn road that led to Gramma's house. The speckled chickens scrambled for safety as he parked near the smokehouse, and a few scrawny dogs immediately came over to meet the new arrival. I felt cautious around him, but I noticed the ease with which he stretched his legs and yawned. Gramma came out of the house, her apron tied neatly around her waist, and hugged him for a long time. Her eyes were closed, and she smiled with a self-satisfied chuckle and patted his back repeatedly.

The days passed. He rose early and stayed up late. He played games with his nieces and nephews that left them giggling and out of breath. He offered to help Gramma before she even asked. He was someone I didn't know, and I felt oddly disarmed by this unfamiliar version of him. I didn't feel deceived or manipulated, just stunned.

Gramma, Dad, and I spent the next two weeks of that summer visiting kin, picking potatoes, repairing Gramma's front porch, cutting grass, and so forth. One day, we went over to the mining hole at Gouge Rock, a place covered in blinding white granite, at the base of which flowed a fast-cold river—the same river Anna and I nearly drowned in when Dad tried to teach us how to swim in 1969. He and Gramma and I made it to the top of Gouge Rock, sweating and breathing heavily. Once there, a cool, wet breeze blew onto my skin. Looking many feet down, I prompted Dad to point out deer tracks in the mud and tell stories about coming there as a child.

Grampa was one of the miners who dug this hole, about sixty feet in diameter at the top of this ridge. Leaning over the edge, I saw several large red oak trees at the bottom. Miners, including my Grampa, carried the waste from this hole on their heads or shoulders and dug downward only as much as the inclined, cone-shaped sides could bear, using a narrow, spiral track to remove the earth. The marks of tools were still visible on the sides, and the earth was still loose.

Dad explained that mica was used in sheet form for stoves mostly, and for glazing. It was also punched into disks and washers as an insulating material in electrical machinery. It was even used in wallpaper. Dad's family said that it was mica what killed Grampa at the age of sixty-three. No one really minded his passing, though; he was saved on his deathbed.

"You best be careful. We used to come here without our mommas knowing where we were," Dad said, looking at Gramma.

"How old were you?" I asked.

"Younger than they should've been," she said.

"What would have happened if Gramma knew you were here?" I asked, curious what he would say.

"She would have whooped us senseless."

"Did anyone ever fall?" I asked.

"Nope, but we sure came close a few times. Especially when we felt like being tough with each other."

"What do ya mean?" I asked.

"Brothers fighting, is all. Linzey and Thomas were the worst."

"Bet they'd say you were," I teased him, finding it hard to believe that any of them could have been worse than him.

"But they'd be wrong," he said, with finality.

One night, about a week before my visit ended, Dad went into the yard and drank some water from the spring that ran down the mountain. There was plenty of moon-blue light as I watched him reach for the ladle that Gramma kept hanging in the apple tree above where the water pooled.

He said to Gramma and me, "I've got a hankering to go a' walking up this mountain. Either of you got the notion to join me?" The longer he stayed at home, the more like a Southerner's his speech became.

I hadn't been alone with Dad in over six years, and his question caught me off guard. And even before he'd come down, I'd become far less afraid than I had been my whole life. Since his arrival, I'd grown to see him more as a whole person than just someone who happened to be my dad. Listening to stories Gramma and his siblings told me about what a responsible son and big brother he'd been, I began to see him as someone who acted the way he did based, in part, on how he was raised, including how his own dad had treated him. I had discovered a gentle side to him in the way he interacted with my cousins. I didn't resent him, which surprised me. I began to understand something about my own suffering that might lend itself to healing.

I also felt the need to prove to him and myself that I was less afraid. If I couldn't be alone with him in the woods at night, then I wouldn't be able to do anything I wanted in my life. I sensed that getting what I wanted would entail not believing my fears about what I could and couldn't accomplish. So, in that moment, I dared myself to go with him to free myself from the burden of this fear, not fully anticipating the gains or losses of such a decision.

I might have said, "I'll go with you. Just let me get my sweatshirt." Or maybe I just asked him, "Which way should we go?" In one memory, I saw myself pointing to the south side of the house, and I began walking. The hill was cow pasture when he was a boy, but it had become overgrown with oak trees, cucumber magnolias, and briar bushes.

Moonlit Walk

We walked in silence most of the way up and stopped only to catch our breath. The slope of the mountains was steep, and though I'd grown used to hiking uphill, it was nice to pause and listen to the sounds of night. I tried to imagine the mountains covered with American chestnuts that, I'd learned from Gramma, were found all along the Appalachian Mountain range back in the late nineteenth century. The chinquapin, a cousin to the chestnut, was one of the only nut-bearing trees still growing in these hills. The katydids sang their washboard song into the night, and the male fireflies speckled the fir trees with their well-lit charm. At one point, I placed my hand on the body of a young birch and felt something cold and wet on my palm.

I yelled out, and Dad stopped with me. He had a flashlight and shined it where my hand was. I stared at the largest slug I'd ever seen, and it was still alive and moving. Its head was raised off the bark of the tree, and it looked ready for a fight.

I felt both disgusted and fascinated, as I had that day he took me catfishing, and I realized that I had barely any memories of going anywhere with Dad when we wouldn't discover something out of the ordinary. Whether it was turning over a rock under which lay a large, green-backed, yellow-bellied garden snake whose sleep had been disrupted or rustling some autumn oak leaves to come across a toad headed toward a mysterious destination, Dad reveled in surprising us this way. Or he'd bring creatures home to us that he found on the highway or near truck stops—dogs mostly, but every now and then something more bewildering. The large snapping turtle is a sharp memory. After he brought it home for us girls to play with, it got loose in our basement. We found it—eventually—underneath the water heater. Then there was the opossum. Not a dead one, mind you. His plan was to bring it back to the woods. My friends and I managed to get it into a bucket and transport it, snarling and hissing, to a wildlife refuge near our home. The funny thing was, when we finally set it free, it simply sat there and stared at us for a good, long minute and then waddled off, not a bit fazed by the ordeal.

Dad and I reached the top of the mountain and sat on some tree stumps in the shadows. I stared at the large undersides of cucumber magnolia limbs. Suddenly, we heard the sound of a whippoorwill nearby, the well-known three parts, "WHIP-poor-WEEA," with a rising last note and first and last syllables accented. Dad and I look toward a log at the edge of the small clearing and neither of us spoke. Dad took out the flashlight for the second time and shined it toward the direction of the sound. Light reflected from the corneas of two pairs of eyes.

"They must be nesting," he said. "They use the light of the moon in their courtship with one another."

"That call is beautiful. I can't imagine being raised around that noise and wanting to ever leave it."

"Well, they weren't the only sounds I heard."

"What do you mean?"

"You seem like you've enjoyed being here," he said.

"It's been good, but I don't like how Gramma pretends to be all good and then judges everybody so harshly, especially Mom." I wanted to talk more about other sounds and how they might have contributed to his leaving North Carolina when he was sixteen.

"That's been true for a long time now," he said.

"But you don't tell her she's wrong."

"What good would that do?"

"I don't know. It would let her know whose side you're on."

"It's got nothing to do with sides," he said.

"Doesn't it? Mom knows you don't defend her. That you go along with everything Gramma says by not challenging her."

"What do you think?"

"I don't know. Everyone has a dark side."

Silence. I hadn't meant to imply anything, but it came out.

"I'm truly grateful for your being here," he said after a moment.

"Why?" I pulled the sleeves of my jacket down around my hands and folded my arms around knees. My bottom felt a little uncomfortable sitting on the stump, but I didn't care.

"'Cuz there's nothing I've done to deserve it and yet . . . "

"It's not for you that I did it."

"I know that."

"Why'd you leave North Carolina if you love it so much? It seems like the place you're most yourself."

"I had to; there was nothing for me to do here to make a living. And my dad was a hard man to be around."

"But you seem happier when you're here."

"In some ways." He stretched his legs out and leaned back toward the heavens. "It's always easier being somewhere that you don't have to work. There's no stress. Like a lot of men, I can be a good man for a little while."

"Do you think you did bad things to Mom and us kids because of how you were raised?" I asked him, hoping my question didn't sound accusatory. We were talking to one another honestly. I wasn't afraid, and he wasn't antagonistic.

"Nah. We make our own decisions despite what happens to us. My brother are good examples. They didn't get raised no differently than me," he said, and paused as if to say something else, but didn't. Instead, he put his head in his hands like a warrior taking a rest.

"Maybe we're not the only ones deciding," I said. "You did some bad things to us. You do know that?"

"I do."

"I worried before coming here, back to where you were born and raised, that I was broken forever."

"I was worried I might have broken you."

"For what you did?"

"That, and for who I was."

The words, shot like an arrow, from a quiver of wisdom: what everyone in my family would love to hear, finally spoken.

"I should feel afraid of you. I could easily hate you!"

"Why don't you?"

"I don't know. I don't think you can really hurt me anymore. I know you won't hurt me here."

In some ways, feeling safe with him where he felt safe made me think how Mom had cut her nose off to spite her face. But I wasn't his wife and I couldn't predict, even now, how he'd behave into the future. And even if he had changed and become the best husband in the world, how would she ever be able to reconcile the difference in him?

We both got up, and he said, "Best be getting back home."

I called Mom when we got back to Gramma's and told her about my decision to return to Somerville, as I'd been seriously considering staying on into the school year.

"My flight will get me in on the thirtieth," I said, genuinely feeling excited about returning. In some unexpected way, the experience of being with Dad had left me lighter.

"When do you think your dad will leave?" she asked me.

"The day after me, but he'll be driving, so it'll take a few days."

"How's he been?"

I felt suddenly irritated. "Different."

"You mean better."

"Yeah, I do mean better."

"It must be nice to go somewhere and be waited on hand and foot."

She said this so bitterly, I felt taken aback. Was she talking about Gramma or me? Or Dad? I didn't want to feel disconnected from her, so I gave her the benefit of the doubt. "Yeah, men do have it nice down here."

"As long as they've been treating you well," she said, now sounding conciliatory herself.

"I should probably go soon. I'll be glad to see everybody. Is Peter up? I wouldn't mind saying goodnight to him."

"He's in bed and watching *The Love Boat*," she said. "We'll be happy to see you." I heard relief in her voice, swelling like a sponge. "Your sisters and brother thought you might just move down there for good."

For a while there, that did seem possible. But I knew it would never really work out for me to stay. I missed my family and my life back home. And school was going to start in a few days. I knew I couldn't keep living with Gramma and keep my sanity, let alone be myself. There were so many ways I didn't fit in.

Before getting on the plane to return up North, I stood looking at the runway through a large window and pressed my face against the glass. I thought about the mica hole, dark and cool, despite the intense heat. I wanted to find a place like that in myself: intact, replenishing, and separate from the world. What if that was what I needed to do? Not acquire the place untouched, but recover it? Remember that it was not lost, just mislaid. I'd been feeling that I'd been robbed of my complete self. What if I could retrieve it? Was there such a thing? Could one recover a part of herself? What if the only reason I didn't know it was with me was that it had been concealed? Could I truly get it back?

My journey to North Carolina created an opening to an emotional mineshaft, filled with unknown recesses and perilous ledges. My reasons for leaving Buckskin seemed like Dad's in some basic ways. I was, in fact, the age he was when he left, though as I learned later in my life, he had far more to escape from.

I hoped that I wouldn't carry on what seemed like generations of violence and denial. But I didn't know, and I felt uneasy about the way that Dad and I seemed alike. He didn't grow up planning to act unjustly; I was certain of that. Why did I think I'd be any different? Maybe the constant fear I had of being the bad girl would be the price I'd have to pay. I didn't know. And like a lot of people, growing up does not happen in a straight line. We detour, get lost, do things that make it hard for us to move forward.

1981

Kicked Out

A mockingbird woke me up. My first thought of the day was, did he have his own song, or was it always somebody else's?

Raising one eyelid ever so slightly, I watched the light in the sky change from navy blue to pastel orange as the sun rose above the two-story houses that lined my parents' street. Pain pounded against my skull from the inside out. I lay on the enclosed front porch of my parent's house, shivering even though all the storm windows were down. I hadn't considered the weather when I made my decision to stay out past my curfew, wearing only a sweatshirt and blue jeans. Or maybe I had, but I hadn't really believed that Mom would follow through on her threat to lock the door.

It was hard to remember a time when Mom and I weren't opponents, but I could still do it if I tried. Like this one time, when I was little, and we lived in North Carolina: June bugs descended upon my sisters and me in the backyard, hundreds of them—chunky brown beetles about three quarters of an inch long with yellowish wings that stuck out untidily from their shiny covers. The three of us fired questions at her. "What are they, Mommy? Where do they come from? Why are they so big?" My brother stood in the shade of the carport. His skin was fair and freckled; he was getting ready to soak us with the hose as he leaned on his crutches.

She wistfully said, "They're June bugs." I imagine she might have been thinking about her own childhood. One that was less fraught with fear than our childhood. One that smelled like homemade wine and sounded like mandolin music.

"Here, take these outside and see how many you can catch in one motion."

She handed each one of us big plastic bags that we shook out excitedly. When we succeeded in capturing them, they blundered dizzily against the walls of their makeshift containers.

I loved Mom purely in these moments, and I would have sworn she was the best mom in the world to anyone who asked. Not the mean mom she became sometimes when she was mad at Dad. Not the pensive mom she became when we didn't know where Dad was. Not the negligent mom who allowed Dad to take me to secluded places. The best mom in the world.

This morning, the latch turned. I was the bad girl again, pretending to be asleep.

"What is wrong with you?" she asked, standing over me. "You can't come home any hour of the night or day." Her terrycloth nightgown was zipped all the way up to her chin.

"I bet you feel good about yourself for not letting me in." I rolled up onto my knees and stretched like a cat with my head bowed to the floor, shoulder-length brown hair falling over my face.

She didn't say anything for a moment, then mumbled, "It's just not right, Rose-Marie. Ever since you came back from North Carolina, you act like you're the one making all the rules. What happened to you?"

I didn't know what had happened to me. I, too, was blindsided by how much more difficult things were between my family and me since I'd returned home. I fought with Mom nearly every day, about everything from her decision to send me to Catholic school to talking about the weather too much. I was angrier with Dad than ever and I kept my distance from Anna and Christina as much as possible. They would try to ignore me back, but I knew my coldness hurt them and their pain made me feel good. It felt good to hurt everyone—except at night, when my fears came to the surface, fears I never revealed to anyone in my family.

I tried to talk about all this with Ella, but that didn't change how I felt. Initially, I was shocked how my connections with my family were deteriorating, but then my feelings began to shift. I felt freer. I continued to do well in school, but Dad's attempts to be the parent he never was pissed me off to no end. I used his past crimes as an excuse for my rage every chance I could get.

When I didn't answer her, Mom said, "Get in the house. I'm not going to tolerate this kind of behavior anymore."

"Why's that, Mom?" I said, standing up on the porch. "Because we have standards in our house? I forgot!" I walked by her into the house.

I smelled percolated coffee and toasted Italian white bread. She'd been up for a while eating her breakfast and not letting me in. Bitch!

"Go to your room," she hissed, "and stop making so much noise or you'll wake up the whole house. It's Sunday, for the love of God!"

"I don't care!" I yelled at full volume, stomped up the stairs to my bedroom, and slammed the door behind me. This, I think, was the moment I decided that I would leave. I didn't know where I'd go, really, but I had a hunch that Jeannie might come to my rescue.

Jeannie and I had been attending St. Clement together for eleven years and hanging out more since starting high school. She ran with a rough crowd by Catholic school standards and, the previous spring, had introduced me to getting high and drinking. After coming back from my trip down South and getting over the fear that I would instantly turn into a drug addict because of my family history, I began to take pleasure in the way mind-altering substances made everything more fun, and funnier.

"I need boys," Sister Dorcas jumped out of her seat and yelled to the class. She had accidentally dropped a giant glass thermometer that we were going to use to measure the temperature of some boiling liquid in some experiment. Silver balls rolled across the floor amidst the pieces of shattered glass.

"I need boys," she said, striding up and down the aisles where we all sat.

Right away, I could feel Jeannie laughing through the floorboards. She sat in the seat directly behind mine. We'd smoked a joint at lunch—there was no way we were going to last through the entire double period Chemistry class without one. With one hand over her mouth, she said, "As do we all, Sister."

Sister Dorcas, with her keen radar for mockery, looked right at us. We were clearly having too much fun, and she came over to where I sat on the far-left side of the lab, said, "Is something funny?" and poked me hard in my left shoulder.

"Ow!" Ever since the car accident, my shoulder was sensitive.

Jeannie burst out laughing.

Before Sister could kick us out, we stood up with our books and left. We could hear our classmates having fun with the unpredictable movement of the mercury balls that were now more scattered across the floor.

Yeah, Jeannie might help me out.

I slept nearly the whole day. I remember Christina, now fourteen, coming into my room and trying to coax me awake. She wanted to go to Harvard Square and "people watch," something she often did on a Sunday afternoon, and wanted me to come along. I kept my eyes closed until she gave up. Even though I knew my response was mean, I didn't feel like I could help myself. All the clarity I had in North Carolina seemed long ago and far away, out of reach, even.

Kicked Out

While everyone sat down to supper that night, I snuck out of my room and did the same thing I'd done the night before. This time, I met up with Jeannie and a couple of her guy friends, of which she had many. We went to the house of a friend whose parents were purported to be away for the long weekend. We sat around drinking beer and smoking pot and cigarettes. Black Sabbath blasted out of the stereo, and I let myself disappear in the smoke and the apathy and the words.

We played poker for hours, got drunk, stoned. Two in the morning, everyone yawning and nodding off. Well, not everyone. This one guy, Tony Manzelli, a little older than the rest of us, was the older brother of Jeannie's current boyfriend. He placed his arm across my shoulders and whispered in my ear, between shots, what a good fuck I'd make. Luckily, Jimmy Balboni, also a classmate from school, offered to stand watch over me as long as I slept on the kitchen table. I don't know what would have happened if he hadn't been there. I wasn't conscious of putting myself in harm's way. I wanted it to be okay to escape in the smoke and sour smell of beer spills. I wanted it to be safe. I wanted something I wouldn't find at this house or any house for some time to come.

It was already morning when I arrived home, so I crashed on the front porch again. Dad joined Mom when they unlocked the door, and they looked down at me like I was a carcass Scruffy had left there. They were probably acting the way they'd been advised to act by Dr. Yaffe. It all seemed so staged, I wanted to vomit.

I got up before either one of them spoke, ran to my room, and began packing. Underpants, bras, socks, one more pair of painter's pants, some T-shirts—all cotton and long-sleeved.

"Where do you think you're going?" Dad stood in the doorway to my room, a human wall.

"I'm leaving, I can't stand it anymore!"

"She's not going anywhere." Mom stood beside him. "Tell her, Ned. Tell her she's not leaving until we say so. Act like her father for once!"

"Don't even try to convince me that way!" I was so furious, I thought I might pass out with the ringing in my ears. "He's not my father. He never has been! He never will be!"

"You're not going," he said calmly.

"I am and there's nothing you can do about it! I don't have to leave now. I can wait as long as it takes. And when you get tired of keeping me your captive, I'm gone for good!"

Just like the old days, Dad reached for his belt. I had won. He'd reverted to his old ways. I saw it in his eyes. Dad had changed a lot, but it didn't matter, not when his back was against the wall.

"Ned, don't!" Mom screamed. She knew Dad was going down the wrong path.

"No, Ned, don't!" I repeated with complete contempt.

"Go on, then!" he yelled. "Get out of here! You're not leaving; we're kicking you out."

I started to laugh. First to myself, and then louder, as I descended the stairs to the front door.

"Come back, Rose-Marie." Mom was crying. "It doesn't have to be like this. We've been through the worst of it. Why do this to us? To yourself?"

I felt nothing. I hated both of them. I couldn't believe I didn't think of this option sooner.

Peter hummed in his bedroom on the first floor. Probably twirling his hair on his forehead.

There was a little girl who had a little curl
Right in the middle of her forehead.
When she was good, she was very, very good
And when she was bad, she was horrid!

Kicked Out

■ — — ■

Christina and Anna sat on the top of the stairs, looking down at me. I knew they were sad to see me go. I did feel something toward them; I felt horrible. I knew in my gut they were losing me as an ally in the constellation of "kids against Dad." I hated the way it affected Peter the most, because whatever he felt, whatever he understood, what he might have wanted to do, he couldn't. He was completely dependent on my parents and probably would be his whole life.

As I opened the door, Scruffy tried to get out. He wanted me to take him with me, but I couldn't. He was getting old, and I didn't know where I might end up. I picked him up to say goodbye and rubbed my face into the top of his head. When I set him down, I told him to stay, and he cocked his head in anticipation that I might take him with me.

I went over to Jeannie's house. It was still early on a Monday holiday, and everyone was asleep. So I sat on her front steps and chewed on my fingernails. When I heard her folks talking in the kitchen, I knocked on the front door.

"Rose-Marie, what are you doing here? It's not even nine o'clock."

"I'm sorry to bother you, Mrs. Summers. Is Jeannie home?"

"I think so. I heard her come in not that long ago."

"Do you mind if I go wake her up? It's kind of important. And can I use your bathroom, Mrs. Summers?"

"Sure."

I peed and then went and told Jeannie what had happened.

"You're staying," she said emphatically.

"Will it be okay with your mom and dad?"

"Oh, definitely." She reached over and grabbed a pack of smokes from her nightstand. She lit one and handed it to me.

"I don't want it. Won't your parents get mad?" I still couldn't believe how much she could get away with compared to me.

"No, they almost lost my older brother by being too strict. They're not going to risk it with me. Besides, I caught my dad getting stoned with Mr. Balboni. I can use that anytime I want."

"Well, she'll have to call my mom. Otherwise, the police will be here before you know it."

"No problem."

Jeannie talked with her mom and she called my mother. I could hear Mom crying through the receiver, and Mrs. Summers nodded sympathetically, then waved at me to go in the living room and watch TV.

Jeannie was watching *Bosom Buddies*, a show about two men pretending to be women so they could live in an all-women house and pay dirt cheap rent.

"This is shit! How can you watch this stuff?" There was an open can of SpaghettiOs on a TV tray next to her chair. I began eating them out of the can.

"What'd your mom say?"

"I don't know for sure; I guess I can stay. I'll have to go back and get some more things. I don't even have a toothbrush."

"You can borrow one of mine."

I dropped down on the couch and aimed my eyes at the stupid show, doing my best to act nonchalant. But I felt both terrible and hopeful. I needed to leave my family, to save myself, but I felt preoccupied with the idea that I couldn't escape my destiny as a bad girl, the kind of girl who has nothing going for her and wastes her life attempting to (unsuccessfully) escape, going nowhere, and pretending (always) that it didn't matter. I'd read stories, lots of them, about girls who were fated to unwittingly repeat their lives, and they'd all been sexually abused. No one I admired had a history like mine. Other people in my family, older cousins, were real-life examples of the kind of young woman I felt doomed to become if I didn't start making some different choices. Mom's goddaughter had a baby taken away from her when she got pregnant, so when she got pregnant a second time, she split and ran off with a loser who left her high and dry. Mom's other goddaughter, Jackie, also got messed up, abusing drugs and getting expelled from school as soon as she turned sixteen. Her parents tried to figure out how to help her and failed most of the time.

Jeannie didn't share my concerns. She embraced the thrill of hanging out with people who obviously didn't have our best interests in mind and doubly enjoyed the effects that various drugs had on her psyche. That night, I crawled into her bed and told her more about my family than I ever had, including the sexual abuse. I also confided that I didn't think I had much of a chance at becoming someone of great consequence, let alone responsible for my own life. "You never know what makes you who you are, Rose-Marie," she said. "I found out a just recently that my brother and I were adopted. We don't even have the same biological parents."

"How come you didn't tell me?" I sat straight up in bed, searching her face for the mother she'd never known.

"You never told me about your dad. Not really."

"Fair," I said, and lay back down, feeling close to her.

"My biological mother fucked up, and I don't care what her reasons were. That doesn't mean I have to fuck up." She paused and then added almost in a whisper, "But it's not a great way to come into this world."

"You mean as a mistake?" I asked, hoping I wasn't saying the wrong thing. She was being so open, and her family was so kind for taking me in. I didn't want to say anything that might hurt her.

"Yeah, and then I was in some orphanage for a few months. A fucking orphanage!"

I realized then that she was crying. I reached for her hand under the covers and grabbed it, holding it tight in my own. I imagined us as a single life, connected and whole. Looking back, I remember this moment as one of the most mutual and loving. Two single lives connecting, and out of that union, replenishing ourselves in a way that felt healing and emboldening. Sharing painful details of my life reduced my shame, and in so doing, increased my sense of worth. I don't remember how long it took us to fall asleep as much as how well I slept that night.

I went back home at the end of the week to get more of my things—and because of Scruffy. Mom had called on Wednesday to tell me she was going to have to put him to sleep. She and Anna, fifteen years old, had been dealing with his having more seizures and pooping all over the house. I had been ignoring the whole problem for months and felt guilty as hell.

He was having a seizure when I arrived, lying on the kitchen floor, his small body twitching like someone had put his paw in an electric socket.

Mom was sitting on the floor near him. "He's okay. Let him finish it out and then he'll stand up on his own."

"How can you watch him do this every day?" I was stunned with how violent it looked.

"I don't have a choice," she said. "I worry he'll hurt himself if I leave him alone."

"Somebody has to take care of him," Anna said hotly. She was trying to lure me back home the best way she knew how.

I wasn't going to fall for it. "I can't. Do what you need to do," I said, and reached down to where Scruffy lay; he licked my hand. Tears fell on his black curly hair, and I thought about all the times I'd used him as a blanket.

"He's been your dog since we brought him home," Mom said. "You owe it to him." She looked at Anna in a way that indicated they had planned this strategy.

Kicked Out

"Yeah, we're all owed something," I said.

I left a few minutes later, wishing I had a joint. Jeannie would have one. I could get stoned with her and everything would feel better. I did get high many times after that; sometimes it helped. Often it didn't. It took a while for my life to mend. To realize that there was more to being alive than re-injuring oneself.

Richard

The room was poorly lit. He sat on an old desk chair with one squeaky wheel, his legs crossed at the ankles. His belt was still unbuckled, and the top button of his tan corduroys dangled loosely. The soft, chocolate brown flannel shirt that he wore over a plain white T-shirt was untucked and wrinkled.

"I can't believe you've never heard of Leonard Cohen," he said to me, but really to himself.

I remember kneeling on the floor in front of him. He leaned over the counter of the video playback station, both of his elbows resting on the blemished pinewood of the countertop so that his upper arms appeared cut and strong, and began fiddling with the receiver, a cigarette hanging from the side of his mouth. He squinted; I couldn't tell if it was because of the smoke that drifted over his head or because his eyesight was waning. At thirty-two years old, he'd been losing hair for some years now and in this light, the bald spot looked like a small, light colored kippah.

The first time Richard brought me to bed—his bed, the bed that he and his wife shared—I was seventeen, and he was fifteen years older than me. It surprised him that I was still (technically) a virgin. We had sex, but never intercourse, and that set the tone for our relationship. Sometimes, especially when we had access to only the front seat of his truck, we'd both get so turned on while we were kissing and touching that we'd often climax with all our clothes on. Other times, he went down on me. When he'd rise up to kiss me, I could smell myself on his beard. Did his wife, Cathy, ever smell me? I wondered, but never asked.

Tonight, I whispered in the shadows, "I can't do this anymore."

"Can't do what?" he said. "There, I got it. You have to listen to this song. Leonard does an amazing job describing the surrender of self that we all have to experience if we want to stop being the hero of our own dramas." I didn't understand what he was talking about. Who needed to stop being the hero? And when did Richard surrender to anyone other than in bed?

"I can't see you anymore." My voice quavered. "And have sex with you and not tell anyone. I . . . I feel like I'm losing my mind."

I raised my eyes in the same moment that he closed his. The words from "The Story of Isaac," majestic and convoluted, filled the room.

He looked down at me. We were in a small, VHS recording studio on the second floor of a three-story Victorian, part of a private, non-profit, multi-media arts studio and youth program, SMAP. Richard was the director of this organization, which served the community and the five hundred or so young people that came through its doors on an annual basis. He was one of the group's founding members.

"You got to relax, Rose-Marie," he said. "Wanna smoke a joint?"

I tried to believe that it could be that simple and sat back, using the sleeve of my sweatshirt to wipe my face. My palms were sweating, and I wiped them on my blue jeans. My bra lay crumpled on the floor in the corner and I moved to put it on, then decided to simply fold it and put it in my back pocket.

"I wish I didn't feel like this. I try to believe you. But I—" A hiccup escaped from my chest, and I blushed. "I keep feeling terrible."

He slid off the chair onto the floor, leaned back against the wall, and pulled out a joint. "Stop judging yourself. You're negating the positive energy of the experience we just had. There's nothing more important than allowing yourself to feel pleasure with another human being who is feeling it too. Life is for having fun. It's all a playground, and you're in my section of it." He had me up until the last sentence. And then from somewhere inside, with a voice sounding a lot like my Mom's, I heard, *He is so full of shit!*

My mother had recently showed up at SMAP furious at Richard, suspicious of his relationship with me, although I had never told her a single detail of what was going on. Trying to protect in ways she hadn't beforehand.

"I'm not letting you in, Mom." I glared at her below the exit sign at the back entrance, but the stare covered a state of panic. The last thing I wanted was my mother barging into this place. I was in trouble, but I hated the thought that Mom would be the one to rescue me. How dare she? Did she think that saving me now would make up for not saving me then?

"There's no way you can stop me. I'll stand here all day."

She looked at me with the most determination I'd ever seen yet in those dark, Italian eyes. Where did she suddenly get the balls to come here? Maybe if I ridiculed her, she'd leave.

"What do you think you're going to do? Richard is the director, Mom! He runs the place the way he wants. He doesn't have to answer to anyone, especially someone like you." Today, I don't know if I meant, because she was nobody to him, or because I didn't see her as powerful or if I just wanted to demean her as a way to enact revenge on her for daring to act like she was concerned for my safety.

"I'm not going until I speak to him. You're my daughter, and I know in my heart of hearts what he's up to."

"He won't admit to a thing, Mom. He doesn't have to. Everyone loves him. I love him!" I knew that scared her, my saying how I felt for him, and I didn't care. I wanted her to leave and, in my naiveté, I thought that emphasizing my fervor would somehow dissuade her from doing what she came to do.

"His charm might work on you, Rose-Marie, but you're still my daughter. I don't have to repeat the mistakes I made when you were a child. Now get out of my way!" And she stormed in, demanding to see him.

He met with her in his disorganized and small office, and though he didn't say much, I could tell he knew she meant business. Immediately afterwards, he began to act cooler towards me. Initially, I was furious at her for that.

Kneeling on the floor, I was even more furious because I could see she'd been right. I felt enraged at him, too, and at myself for being made a fool. Furious at all the hippie happy talk that he'd used to justify our relationship—and all the other relationships he had or was having. It was a badly kept secret among the teens who visited the studio that we were all—girls and sometimes even boys—in his playground. I was just another set of swings.

I ran out of the room and out of the building. It was after midnight, and the moon was completely covered in thick, dark clouds. I stumbled through the dark streets muttering, "What a fucking idiot I am!"

I asked myself over and over how I got myself into this mess. But I knew. I knew it in that mysterious and untold part of myself, where I'd been squirreling away uncomfortable knowledge my whole life. But that secret memory bank was now full, and about to overflow.

In one memory I have of that night, I collapse against a brick wall and begin to weep. And there is no way I can stop it. In another memory, I stand over the subway vent outside Davis Square and pace, smoking one cigarette after another. In yet another memory,

I crawl into my bed and scream into a pillow until my throat is raw and my tears burn my cheeks.

I'd met Richard through Jeannie. For months, she'd been telling me about both Richard and the program, Somerville Media Action Project (SMAP). She made it all sound very intriguing and dicey.

"You're gonna love this place, Rose-Marie."

"Why's that?

"'Cuz nobody there treats kids as less important than adults. Everyone is equal. You don't even have to wear shoes if you don't want," Jeannie said, knowing how much I enjoyed being barefoot.

One afternoon, curiosity finally got the better of me, and I stopped by the storefront they were operating out of to meet up with her. I walked into what had once apparently been a grocery store; the outlines of shelving units were still visible on the tiled floor. But instead of racks of chips and Cocoa Puffs, there were shoeless and skinny teenagers, long hair hanging in their faces, wearing blue jeans and AC/DC t-shirts, sitting on beat-up desktops and boxes filled with paint supplies and emulsion products for the silk-screens that needed to be cleaned. It seemed everyone was smoking, and lyrics of "Another Tricky Day" by The Who bellowed out of someone's tape deck.

I fell in love with the place, so different from my home or school, so welcoming of kids who didn't fit the mold.

"Come on." Jeannie led me over to a group of kids milling around what I later learned was an old photo offset printing press.

One of them, smoking a joint that looked nearly as narrow as a toothpick said, "I don't get why he's so popular."

Jeannie leaned over to me and whispered, "Reagan." I was impressed that she knew that without having to ask.

Another kid said, "Just because someone tries to kill you shouldn't make you a fuckin' hero!" and then danced across the room playing air guitar the way Jim Morrison did at Woodstock.

Richard

"Everyone didn't become a democrat when Kennedy was shot," another kid said.

Except that he wasn't a kid. I realized that this was one of the grownups in the room. Then, as I watched, he reached over, plucked the joint from the first kid's fingers, took a long drag, and handed it back. This was not like anywhere else I'd ever been.

The kid took the joint back. "Thanks, Richard. And what the fuck do drugs have to do with anything?"

"They won't be the only ones going after drugs, hard, soft or otherwise," air guitar said. "There's a long line in front of them! I saw Costa in it last week. He was there with his buddy, 'King God Fuck,' and the two of them would have been hard pressed to give up their spot. Running up the battle flag ain't the way to win this war!"

Air guitar was answering joint guy, but he was talking to all of us as if he were on stage. We all laughed and shook our heads, including the grownup, Richard.

I tried to take in this new model of adulthood. I'd had plenty of experience with "youth-serving professionals," with their judgments and rules that seemed more rooted in "us" and "them" distinctions. But Richard didn't seem to pay attention to us/them at all. I felt completely at ease with adults for the first time since Ella, my therapist.

After that day, I started visiting every chance I got, just to be near peers, many of them intelligent and cynical. I rather quickly learned that they were also extremely uneducated—most of them drop-outs—and poor. None of them seemed to have any interest in living past thirty years old, let alone going to college. But despite all of that—or perhaps because of it—I came to feel at home there.

My relationship with my dad was almost non-existent at this point, and my mom and I were constantly fighting. She would claim to be concerned for me but act overly protective in a way that only served to unearth my resentment.

One night, Richard offered to take Jeannie and me swimming.

I was happy to accept; it was one of the hottest summers I could remember and by then I had a serious crush on him. I knew he felt the same towards me. He would touch the small of my back when he needed to move behind me, his face lit up when I came into the room, and he would ask me questions about my life that were probing in a way that made me feel special.

We drove over to The Mystic Lakes that night, the three of us sharing a cigarette in the front seat of the "SMAP Mobile," a beat-up Chevrolet Biscayne wagon. We were anticipating how good the cold, fresh water would feel on our sweat-soaked bodies. Richard, as was his habit, invited Jeannie and me to share stories of life at St. Clements. He seemed especially interested in tales that involved our frustration about what was wrong with our families, school, and the world. He was the first adult I'd met who wasn't defensive when I criticized adults, and we were more than happy to take advantage of the opportunity to grumble. And Catholic school offered lots of opportunities to grumble.

"Sister Dionysus is on the war path," Jeannie whispered to me in geometry one afternoon, before English Literature, which Sr. Dionysus taught.

"What happened?" I asked chewing on my eraser head, waiting for the bell to ring.

"She confiscated a note that Stevie drew . . . " I sighed. Stevie was a six-foot-tall Irish boy who probably weighed 250 pounds. When he wasn't complaining loudly about how burdened he felt by Catholicism, he would draw graphic depictions of the religious staff in compromising positions and share them with his classmates in the form of carefully folded notecards. We all enjoyed it when one started to get passed around the classroom, especially on days when it felt too hot to pay attention to the lesson.

"This one was a doozy," Jeannie said and began to giggle, covering her hand over her mouth.

Richard

"You have to tell me," I demanded.

"He did a stunning depiction of Sr. Dio bent over in front of her shopping cart with Fr. Bergin behind her."

"You mean behind her?"

"Up the butt." I laughed out loud and so did Jeannie and our classmates all turned to see what was so funny. Of all people to discover Stevie's artistic depictions of clerical life.

"Settle down, ladies or else—" Just then, the bell rang.

Catholic school could also feel unbearable to me: constantly obeying an authority outside myself, teachers espousing "blessed are the meek" rhetoric while humiliating students who were less powerful, particularly the girls.

I was holding my arm outside the right passenger window to feel the breeze. "Why don't you tell Richard about how you fell flat on the floor the other day when Father Bergin was talking with you?"

She giggled. "Tell it."

"Okay, see, Jeannie had taken so many Quaaludes that she couldn't stand up." Richard handed me a joint and I took a drag. "The weird thing was Father Bergin didn't say a thing. He looked down at her, then looked at me with his eyebrows raised, then just turned and walked back to his classroom."

Richard was laughing too. "He didn't say anything?"

Jeannie covered her mouth with her hand. "I don't remember any of this."

I said, "He yelled over his shoulder before he went into the room, 'Make sure I see you both in fifth period.'"

"Ah," Richard said. "The obligatory assertion of authority."

I looked sideways at Jeannie. "It was so ridiculous. And really unfair."

"What do you mean unfair?" Jeannie asked.

"That I had to make sure you didn't get in trouble or die!"

We all laughed. I don't know really know what made them laugh; maybe because Father Bergin's response was so deficient it was absurd. Or maybe it was the pot. In any case, I still was shocked at some level to be able to tell a story like that to an adult and have him laugh along.

When we got to the pond, Richard parked near some leafy sycamore trees, and we found a small trail that led down to the water's edge. In one memory, Richard takes off all his clothes and dives in. In another he asks, "Ever swam nude before?" And in yet another memory, I stand in the water up to my ankles, smoking a cigarette just as I become aware that Richard is helping Jeannie take off her shirt.

I stare for a moment, then, without speaking, follow suit. While I'd never been skinny dipping, I didn't hesitate. Maybe it was the pot.

Richard swam far out, but Jeannie and I stayed near the small shoreline. A half-moon cast light on our skin making it glow. I felt Richard's hand grasp my ankle before I realized he was near us again. His head popped up in front of me and he reached out and stroked my cheek.

"See those stars?" Richard pointed to a cluster that hung like fruit from a tree. "That's part of the Pegasus constellation."

I leaned my head back in the water and my breasts floated freely to the surface. I wanted to catch sight of whatever he wanted to show me.

When I went back to treading water, Richard swam over so he was next to me. "You're gorgeous in the water."

I felt my heart flutter like a bewildered moth. What was I doing? Who was this man? What was going to happen?

"Come on girls; ride me out a little further."

Jeannie and I put one hand on each shoulder, and it felt like riding a dolphin—or so I imagined. We stayed in the water, having fun splashing each other and playing. Our bodies touched, but nothing sexual happened. At least not that night.

Richard

■ — — ■

I was in the darkroom, after-hours at SMAP, developing black-and-white pictures I'd recently taken of street people in Harvard Square. I enjoyed the red light of a darkroom and seeing my photos go from being invisible to distinct and contrasted.

Richard entered the room quietly and came up behind me. I felt his hard penis brush against my backside at the same moment that he kissed my neck. I felt turned on, in a way that was just like what I remembered from making myself come, powerful and strong. The blood rushing to my lower belly, determined and fixed, made me feel lost and greedy. But I also felt afraid; I'd never had intercourse with anyone and was worried he'd think I had. What to do? But he touched me, and I couldn't resist; I leaned into him and let him cup my breasts in his hands. Woozy and gasping for air, we made out for what seemed like an eternity, but at one point, I pulled myself away from him. "What about your wife? Isn't she upstairs? Won't she wonder where you are?"

"We have to move with our feelings, Rose-Marie, without doubt or trepidation. We've got to take risks, even risks that might result in total annihilation."

I didn't stop to ask how his wife was going to totally annihilate us. I was young and idealistic and turned on, and his language sounded noble and reassuring. I fell in love with him and all that he stood for, right then and there, especially the parts of him that reflected how to live and do good work in the world.

It didn't matter to Richard that he was in the main position of leadership within a program designed to help troubled youth. It didn't matter that he was married and his wife, also quite a bit younger than him, was expecting their first child. It didn't matter that the staff social worker, his first wife, had informed him that I was vulnerable to sexual abuse. None of that mattered to Richard as much as how he felt in the "here and now." And now, I agreed with him, yearning for something so bad that I was willing to trust in anything that might give it to me.

Months passed after that night and soon after the experience at the playback station, Richard told me that it was time for me to move along. At that point, I felt an amalgamation of emotions—hurt, enraged and alarmed for the kids entering the program, who like myself, placed their trust in his hands. What would happen after I left? Wouldn't he just keep doing what he did? What reason would he have to stop? Were there others and why hadn't they come forward?

Instead of quietly taking my leave, I asked around and discovered that I was not the first youth participant in SMAP he had seduced. I also knew that unless I said something, I wouldn't be the last.

Sasha was the first adult I confided in about my relationship with Richard. She was the coordinator of the video department at SMAP. She was also the only other adult on staff older than Richard, and female. When I asked to talk with her, she invited me up to her tiny apartment that overlooked the new subway station in Davis Square. A late autumn rain had started pouring down while I was walking over, and my hair was soaked. I was scared and still wasn't clear about how inappropriate my relationship with Richard was. I had tried to sift through my feelings of rejection so as not to act out of indignation or acrimony.

When I got to her place, I worried about dripping onto her carpet, but she pulled me into the living room, got me a towel, and started the teakettle going in her galley kitchen.

"Don't you have an umbrella?" she said while she set up a tray.

"Well, yeah, but . . . I forgot it. I've got a lot on my mind, I guess."

Richard

She came in and took the seat across from me. "Well, I know you're not here to talk about your hair."

I told her the whole story from the time Richard had talked me into his bed when I was seventeen, and what I'd been able to find out about what had happened to other kids in the program.

In her forties, with jet-black hair cut in a short punk style, she didn't "look" like the type to be upset about Richard's bohemian lifestyle. But I knew she had three daughters of her own, and that she cared about me. As she listened, she went from curious to shocked to enraged.

"Okay, stop," she said when I started to repeat myself. "We have to take this to the board of directors."

"But . . . isn't Richard's wife—"

"And his ex-wife, who is a practicing social worker, by the way, and his father. They're all on the board. It doesn't matter. Believe me, I know them, and they're going to be on your side about this. Besides, they're not going to want this in the papers. Do you think we could get some of the other kids to testify?"

I was stopped by that word, "testify." I realized then that I had been assuming that some of what had been going on was my fault. After all, no one had forced me into his bed. It wasn't like what my father had done.

But now I was no longer so sure.

Sasha was still talking. " . . . arrange a meeting with the board, and I'll bring along a lawyer to explain things to Richard in no uncertain terms. I swear, he's going to be out the door by the end of the week." Suddenly she looked straight at me. "You know, you've done an incredibly brave thing here."

I was aware of my hair still dripping onto her upholstery. I must have looked like a drowned rat. "Brave? What are you talking about?"

"You said there'd been others over the years, right? Why did they all just quietly fade into the underbrush? Why didn't they come forward?"

This brought me up short again. I didn't feel like I was accomplishing something brave. I was just doing what was clearly the right thing to do. For the first time in my life, I told the truth and somebody, an adult, did something about it. That's not quite what I would call bravery, but it got the job done.

While Richard was still in the stage of thinking the whole thing would just blow over and he could remain director of SMAP, he suggested a therapy session and had the gall to ask his ex-wife, the staff social worker, to mediate the conversation between him and me. She agreed for reasons she would later admit were self-interested, and he acted as if most of what had happened between us was rooted in hurt feelings and misunderstandings rather than manipulation and abuse of power. To this day, I don't know if he realized the extent to which his sexual relationships with teens in the program was unscrupulous and corrupt. My childhood therapist Ella, who I'd begun seeing again after leaving him, knew that I would be at a huge disadvantage, talking it out with Richard and Lily, and joined me without asking either one their permission to do so.

I can still see their surprise when we entered the room where Lily met with clients in her home.

Ella proved her worth and her expertise in the first five or ten minutes into the conversation. "What you don't seem to understand is that there is more going on than a break-up gone sour. She was one of the teen participants, for Christ's sake!"

I'd never heard Ella yell nor seen her smoke a cigarette, and she was doing both. "You said yourself that you found out that Rose-Marie was a sexual abuse survivor and had informed Richard of that detail. You're culpable too!" Ella turned to me and asked, "What do you want to do, Rose-Marie?"

Richard

Richard was in denial and afraid, and Lily seemed confused. "I'm sorry that everyone is upset, but I can't take away what happened or my fear that Richard will continue to have sex with kids in the program." Silence, awkward and heavy, followed Ella and I as we left. I made an appointment to see her the next day, just she and I, one-on-one, back to our usual regimen. I was beginning to figure out that the news about my relationship with Richard was rocking other people's worlds. Many of the male members of the board wanted to know the sexual details. When I would see them in the building or on the street they said, "It couldn't have been that bad," or "That doesn't sound too painful, Rose-Marie. Why do you want to bring him down?" I would shake my head and keep walking, wondering to what extent my accusations made them worried about their own behaviors and feeling perplexed by their lack of understanding

I felt afraid and as we gathered three or four of Richard's former lovers to testify against him. But I couldn't have stayed true to myself had it not been for the support of so many people, especially the other teens in the program, who, though not victims in the pure sense, also felt betrayed by Richard. We banded together in our resolve to tell the truth.

In 1984, stories about sexual abuse were rare, at least in the public eye. Given that my situation entailed teens, who often chose and sometimes enjoyed aspects of the relationships, I don't know what would have happened if I'd gone to the papers. Luckily, Ella and other professional staff from the local mental health center and EMERGE—an organization founded in 1977, whose mission was to eliminate violence towards women—became more involved, offering their expertise and support.

It took a few years for the whole thing to play itself out. In all that time, nobody else ever (formally) stepped forward. On the other hand, there wasn't a single young person I spoke to who'd also had a relationship with Richard that didn't endorse my "coming out" with what happened. Surprisingly, most adults who knew Richard weren't shocked. The details of my relationship with him often reminded them of times they'd had their own questions about his boundaries. Why they'd never confronted him or told anyone else about what they'd seen is still somewhat a mystery to me.

Eventually, the board of directors ordered Richard to resign as director. I suspect this outcome surprised no one more than him. He and his wife moved out of SMAP and bought a home one town over. They had more children following their son and were married for many years thereafter. At one point, I found out Richard was working with young people again and I went immediately and told them what happened at SMAP. Richard found out and threatened to sue, but nothing came of it. Truthfully, I had nothing to lose. I didn't have any money, and all I did was tell them the truth.

At first, I grieved over the loss of Richard in my life, but eventually mourning opened up the other losses that needed to be examined. Lamenting with Ella became a way to shed that misery and despair, which I had built into my identity. It also made it possible to continue walking on a path towards recovery and wholeness.

PART THREE

Reconciliation: Latin origin, meaning to make consistent or compatible.

■·—·■

When I talk of forgiveness, I mean the belief that you can come out the other side a better person. A better person than the one being consumed by anger and hatred. Remaining in that state locks you in a state of victimhood, making you almost dependent on the perpetrator. If you can find it in yourself to forgive, then you are no longer chained to the perpetrator. You can move on, and you can even help the perpetrator to become a better person, too.

—Desmond Tutu in The Forgiveness Project

■·—·■

"Where there is reconciliation, Stephen says, there must have been a sundering."

—James Joyce

1988

Three Identical Bracelets

1988. The last year of Reagan's presidency—a gallon of milk cost $1.89, *Graceland* became a major commercial hit despite the controversy Paul Simon faced for breaking the cultural boycott imposed by the rest of the world against the apartheid regime in South Africa, and my sisters and I graduated in unison. I took me six years to get through the University of Massachusetts. Anna went to the same university in five, and Christina attended Clark University in Worcester, Massachusetts, for four years. The year before our commencement, I'd become involved with Students Organized Against Reaganism (SOAR) and felt camaraderie with my fellow students, all of whom felt a certain level of outrage combined with optimism. After a summer of working on a locked psych unit for mentally ill patients, I decided that I couldn't bear becoming a psychiatrist, even though that had become my plan. The field seemed oblivious to the social and economic context in which people led their lives, and the doctors I'd met at Cambridge City Hospital came across as superior and condescending to everyone who didn't have a medical degree. So, I shifted majors in midstream and emerged, after six years, with a dual degree in psychology and philosophy.

The Clash lyrics, bone crunching, rabble rousing, and discontented, pumped out of the speakers that were behind me in a giant club, located near South Station in Boston. It overlooked the channel, and bar patrons could stand on the pier out back and smell freshly prepared sausages with peppers and onions while gazing at the reflection of stars in the water on clear cold nights like this one. It was the week of our shared graduation. I stomped the cement floor with my weathered army boots, hanging out near the dark and smoky bar. The second-hand indigo-blue dress I'd worn to accentuate my womanly figure in military gear was a reasonable costume for this sort of gig. I wasn't accustomed to the soft shoulders, nipped-in waist and full skirt, but it worked to get the attention I pretended not to notice.

"Wanna go outside before the show starts?" my old friend Jeannie asked. We were there to see our favorite live ska band, and it was our habit to time our high with their third song in the first set.

"I don't think we'll need to. This club doesn't mind an occasional toke, especially for a crowd like this one." I swept my arm toward the throng of young music lovers entering the club.

She smiled at me and began looking for something in her purse. "You got any?"

"Sure," I pulled a joint from my wallet, one that I'd been saving for just this moment. I held the lighter for her, and she nodded when it caught.

"You did it, Rose-Marie, you graduated," she said, looking out. "I knew you'd do it. You haven't left, but you've gone. Gone away from it."

"What's the 'it'?" I asked, looking at the ocean below.

"All the crap that you were raised to believe about yourself, that made you feel like nothing," she said. "May you carry the hindsight to know where you've been," she said with an Irish brogue and leaned her head on my shoulder.

Mom hosted a big bash in the backyard. Dad wasn't living with her at the time, and it had become more commonplace for him to be M.I.A. We wondered where he was, but we weren't worried enough to ask. Invariably, he always ended up back home, even if it meant that he'd just missed being present for yet another important milestone in our lives.

On the day of the party, my sisters and I were meant to arrive early and together to help. Sun poured in through the patio doors, and the aroma of coffee and toast greeted me like old friends. I was still feeling stunned that we had all succeeded in our attempt to further our education. I'd worked part time the entire time I was in school, and there were moments I didn't think I'd make it. The workload was too heavy, my rent was too high. I felt deeply satisfied that, despite obstacles, we'd all pulled through. I also hoped that I wouldn't forget my friend Jeannie's words.

"Where's Christina?" I asked, entering the kitchen through the backdoor. I assumed she'd be late, even though we all agreed to arrive at Mom's no later than ten o'clock.

"She called. She'll be here soon," Mom said, wanting to distract me from my annoyance. She stood at the stove as her mother probably did before any large family gathering, adding spices to the meatballs, slicing cucumbers and olives, raising the temperature on the Crock-Pot.

"Where's she driving from?" I asked, leaning my chin on her shoulder and putting my finger in the sauce so I could taste it, simple and delicious.

"Her girlfriend's house," Mom said.

Christina had come out of the closet a few years ago, and I felt proud of Mom for using the term "girlfriend" without hesitation. That didn't come easy for a lot of parents whose children had come out to them.

"Can I use the iron?" I asked, reaching my fingers into a jar of black and shiny Kalamata olives. The table was covered with loaves of bread, drinks, and condiments. My black linen shirt and skirt had fallen off the hanger, and I had to do something about the wrinkles.

"Don't touch any food until you wash your hands. The iron is upstairs and probably still set up from when I used it this morning," Mom said, then turned to Peter and said with affection, "You've got to get in the shower before everyone gets here."

I went up the stairs to what used to be my parents' bedroom and for the last few years had become Mom's. She and Dad didn't sleep together anymore. Her bed was made, and her bureau was covered with shiny costume jewelry that had been Nana's, pictures of smiling children's faces, little pencil-written notes, hand lotions, and a prayer plant that I'd given her years ago. I picked up a small talcum bottle and took a whiff.

I will remember that day as one of the happiest in Mom's life. Outside of the support her parents provided, not many people in her family thought she'd succeed in becoming a nurse and then a lieutenant in the Navy. Many people in our family didn't really support my sisters and me going to school, either. I imagine that our success felt like affirmation for all she had done to get us to this point, and exoneration for her wrongdoings.

I came back downstairs, hands washed and dressed for the party, and said hello to Peter.

"You look beautiful," he told me. I gave him a big hug, and as I attempted to extricate myself from his grasp, I asked Mom, "When do you want me to go for the platters?"

"Soon. I ordered some things that need to stay warm," she said, stirring a red sauce on the stove.

"Mom, it's not going to matter. No one's going to be here for a while, and the food is going to sit out anyway."

Just then, Anna arrived. "Hi, everyone. Did Auntie Ada say she would make it?" she asked, coming in the back door as well. She walked over to where Mom and I were standing and put her face between ours. We kissed her simultaneously on each cheek.

"Of course, she's coming! Why would you think otherwise?"

"Well, she's not coming because of me."

"Oh, stop that!" I said. "Just because she's happy to see all of us graduate doesn't mean she isn't proud of her goddaughter."

"Easy for you to say. You've always had Auntie Gina. Just watch. Auntie Gina will give all of us presents, but you'll get something nicer than what she gives Christina and me. That's what a good godmother does. Auntie Ada will give us all desk sets, I know it."

Anna's boyfriend of two years came in and immediately hugged Anna from behind while grinning as if to say, "I know Anna is grumbling, but don't we love her anyway."

Christina walked in from the front of the house and dropped a big, colorful paper bag on the floor. "The party favors and I are here!" Her hair, cut extremely short with blonde streaks in the front, made her look like a striking, exotic bird.

"When did you do this?" I asked, rubbing my hand on the back of her head.

"A few nights ago. You like?"

"Gorgeous. Now you really look like the baby dyke you are."

"Thanks. Is Cousin Alice coming?"

Peter rolled his wheelchair into the room and then sat folding a piece of paper, just as he did as a child.

"Yes, yes, she's coming too!" Mom said. "Why are you girls worrying so much?"

She was back at the stove sprinkling mozzarella and Parmesan on the chicken cacciatore and eggplant Parmesan. Stuffed artichokes were steaming in the pressure cooker. I went over and watched as she slathered red sauce on top of the eggplant.

I leaned my head on her shoulder, which felt awkward because she was shorter than me. It was new for me to be this affectionate with Mom.

"Smile, girls."

We both turned, and Christina took our picture. She was wearing a formal and flattering cream-colored linen dress with a fluorescent orange feather boa.

"You look so cute!" I said.

I felt overcome with nervousness; warmth between Mom and me was still new. We had gone through some brief mother-daughter therapy with Ella, and it had helped a lot. Mom now took responsibility for not being more of a mother to me, and I acknowledged that a lot of my anger toward Dad had been misdirected toward her. "You know you've made way too much food," Christina said. "What can I do?"

Mom turned. "You've already done it. I'm so proud of you girls."

Soon, most of our cousins, many of whom were older and already married with children, began to arrive. While we ate and hung out with one another, the mood grew festive and celebratory.

"Help me with this umbrella. I can't make it go up," Mom yelled to no one as she stood on the back porch, struggling to provide my brother some shade.

"I do. I do." Peter leaned over to help, and the table tilted so that everyone's plates went sliding off. My cousins Johnny and Freddy helped to steady him.

"Watch out, big guy! Trying to steal the show, huh?" Johnny growled, pretending to be upset.

"Leave him alone," I said, trying to sound casual. I felt slightly protective toward Peter. He didn't have the ability to defend himself, especially if someone was using sarcasm, and my cousins had always been unkind to him.

They backed off, making another joke about Peter being a momma's boy, and I stood beside him for a few minutes, remembering that no matter how much my family cared for one another, they were not to be trusted completely.

Auntie Gina clinked her glass and suggested everyone raise his or hers. "We all know that Rosaria has waited for this day a long time. There was never a doubt in my mind that her girls would succeed. It is with great pride that we honor them today!"

Everyone hooted, and my sisters and I raised our held hands to the cloudless sky above us.

Uncle Larry yelled out, "I still don't know why they need a college degree. Pretty girls like them should have no problem getting married. They should be having babies by now."

"Shut up, Larry," Aunt Gina said. "You have no idea what you're talking about."

A few of my cousins with young children began to leave, and that's when Ella arrived. We anticipated that she might be late, and we were glad to see her.

"Come in, come in," Mom said. "Do you want some coffee? How 'bout some pasta?"

"No, I'm fine. I can't stay, but I wanted to give your girls a graduation present." She handed us small boxes, wrapped in silver paper and tied with a red bow. We opened them simultaneously and each one of us took out a gold-braided bracelet.

"I bought one necklace and asked a jeweler I know to make it into three identical bracelets." She smiled widely as we attached the jewelry to our wrists. The bracelets symbolized our connection to one another and the value of that connection. My sisters and I originated from the same place, but we had simultaneously become also distinct from one another. We would remain unusual in our shared ability to enter one another's lives, a quality that meant our own lives and those of our children would continually overlap and connect. Furthermore, Ella—in particular—given the time she entered our predicament and her sensitive and generous heart— would become the standard by which I would measure others and myself, around many things, but most importantly in valuing how much connection matters.

Dad had missed so many important occasions while I was

growing up, but it didn't prevent me from wishing he was with us that day. It irritated me that I still wanted him around, after having done so much work to accept that it hadn't ever been my own father who was right for that job. The lingering desire for him to be someone he wasn't troubled me, but I brushed my distress aside and went on.

A few weeks later, Mom got a call from Massachusetts General Hospital telling her to come in. Dad had undergone surgery for a sudden angina attack and was in critical condition in the ICU. She called my sisters and me. We agreed to go visit Dad's family.

Together we pushed through the heavy metal doors into the cold room. I rubbed my arms absentmindedly in response to my body's shivers. It would have been cold any season, but August made the temperature even more conspicuous. The nurse on staff told us that he was essentially "on ice." This protocol apparently makes it easier on the body to adjust to the procedure. If all went well, he would be sitting up and talking in a few days.

We slowly approached the gurney where he was lying. The sheet draped over him, along with the white cotton turban wrapped around his head, made him look like a giant mummy. Mom took his hand and didn't even flinch; that's why when I touched his skin, I was so surprised I almost screamed. He was frigid as if he'd just come in from a winter's day, and his face was bloated. Filled with the fluids I could see coming out of the machines that surrounded his body, machines that were doing the work of making sure his chest still rose and fell as he breathed.

"Do you think he knows we're here?" Christina whispered.

"It's possible," Mom said. "I've worked with a lot of patients who seemed completely unconscious of their surroundings, but when they opened their eyes, told me things that they heard and felt." She never took her eyes off Dad.

Three Identical Bracelets

"Is he in pain?" I asked. I don't know why it mattered to me, but I didn't want to believe he was suffering while we stood there watching him.

"You better hope he's not feeling anything," Anna said to no one.

Peter was at the end of the gurney and immediately placed his hand on Dad's ankle. He held his forehead in his hand and wept quietly, which brought us all to tears.

"I had operations before," Peter said. "He be alright."

Over the next few days, each one of us took turns sitting beside Dad. Christina had returned from Clark and was working. Anna was on the verge of moving in with her boyfriend. I'd spent a few years being single and was living in Cambridge near Central Square. I worked as a counselor-teacher at an in-school adolescent health clinic and belonged to a video production group that aired a local live show about political issues and the arts. I loved making plans every night of the week and did my best to enjoy myself as a young single woman. The memory of him lying in the intensive care room that day is the one I will always remember as his "near death" experience. It was the summer of 1988; I was twenty-four and Dad was fifty. I happened to be with him the next morning when he was in a deep sleep.

Was he dreaming? Was he remembering his life? I sat beside him trying to imagine him as a baby. Isn't that what the Dali Lama told me to never forget? No matter our crimes, we're all born into this world innocent and precious. Did Gramma nurse him? When he cried, was he comforted, or did he have to self-soothe? What did he enjoy about being the oldest of seven children? Did it pain him to walk to school barefoot? What reasons did his father have to beat him? When he sat in the cherry tree waiting for Grampa to come back from the war, was he excited or was he scared? How young was he when the men took him off to the still to drink? Did he love the buzz of doing something evil with men, his own daddy included, who didn't believe in going to church? What did it feel like to get saved and be completely submerged in the river?

I wanted to understand what had happened to him as a child that made him grow up and do the things he did. I wanted to remember that he'd been powerless once and would be again. I wanted to see his humanity.

Just then, he managed to open his eyes and threw up a few times into a small basin that I held below his chin. A moan escaped from somewhere deep inside him, and I thought I might be sick, too.

"You don't have to stay here with me," he said.

"I know," I said, unable to say what I was feeling: how I didn't like being with him, but I couldn't imagine being anywhere else. I was genuinely afraid of losing him. He seemed so fragile, although he was still a physically big man, standing over six feet tall and broad shouldered. How come I felt obligated to take care of him? How dare my parents teach me to do something for them that they never did for me? Did he ever regret not coming to my aid when I was sick or injured? Or worse, did he realize just once that I was often wounded because of the abuse he inflicted on me? On all of us?

"Where's your mother?" he asked.

"She's on her way. She'll be glad you decided to come back."

"Was never a choice not to, I got unfinished business to take care of."

I had no idea what that meant, but his face had a slight green cast. He looked like he was going to pass out. It didn't seem like a good time to ask about his true feelings, and I felt afraid of what he might tell me. What if he wanted my forgiveness? What if I didn't want to forgive him? Would things really change? I felt like "Christ on the Cold Stone," a sixteenth-century painting from the Netherlands I'd once seen. I was headed toward something inevitably freeing but frightening, nonetheless. Is that how it works? Do we fear our own death only to discover life on the other side?

1989

Confrontation

Bypass surgery afforded Dad a second chance, and when Anna stipulated that he undergo treatment for being a sexual offender, he didn't resist. He stopped drinking and coincidentally began therapy at EMERGE. Almost immediately, the rapport between him and Mom changed for the better: they ran household errands together, went out for lunch with one another, and shared more in Peter's care. It was like nothing we could have imagined growing up. Occasionally, Dad would even go to a town meeting about some local issue affecting the community. He did the chores that weren't easy for Mom to do. And he would ask us how we were when we would stop by to do our laundry or have supper.

He appeared to be changing, and I wanted to give him a chance. My sisters and I were wary of the extent to which he understood what he claimed to know, and sometimes he would attempt to share aspects of his healing that we didn't understand or that would make us uncomfortable. I believed Dad would still have been a wounded person regardless of his sexual pathology. And each one of us, Anna, Christina, and I, had to figure out how best to respond and move ahead.

A humid breeze, smelling like pennies, blew through the window. The day had finally arrived, and a rainstorm was coming. I sat in the waiting room outside Ella's office. I felt surprisingly composed and folded my hands over the pages from which I was going to read the words I'd carefully written and rewritten over a period of many months. Ella appeared in the doorway with a kind smile on her face.

"Come on in. I thought it would be easier if you were already seated before your parents arrive."

I entered her office for what felt like the zillionth time. This therapy session was long in the making. Ella had suggested a formal confrontation with my parents, and as reluctant as I may have initially felt, the day was finally here. It had taken a long time to prepare myself.

I remembered when Ella had first suggested the idea.

"I'll help you. The way it works is you say what you remember about the abuse, then how it made you feel, and you end with telling them what you want from them now and into the future," she said, looking at me with her warm brown eyes.

"What will they do?" I asked, immediately concerned with some imagined idea of their discomfort. I pictured them like clowns with giant smiles painted on their faces, tilting their heads sideways whenever they heard a word that made them awkward.

"Listen," she said. "Their work will be to listen."

"How do we arrange it?" I asked.

"I'll talk with Dr. Yaffe," Ella said. "She can explain the process to them, and then you can call them, invite them to come." She felt confident that my parents would do anything I asked of them, but it still took a few months before I got up the nerve to call my mother. She answered on the first ring.

"Hey, how are you?" I sat on the edge of my bed with the phone in the crook of my neck.

"We're fine. I'm just putting in a load of laundry."

"Good. Listen . . . I want to know if you and Dad would come to see Ella with me. She thinks a formal confrontation would be helpful to me, to you and Dad, to our family."

There was a pause before she spoke, and I gazed out my bedroom window located on the third floor of an old Victorian split-level in Cambridge. A man dressed in a black martial arts outfit was moving a large, gold sword in circles around his body on the basketball court. He seemed confident and graceful. I imagined myself as the sword in his hands.

"Yes," she said after what felt like a long time. "Your father and I are doing our best to receive guidance. We trust Dr. Yaffe more than anyone else."

I wondered what she looked like on the other end of the phone line. Was she scared? Did she really understand my question?

"You'll go through with it, then?"

"Of course. We both will."

The man on the court started swerving his body away from an imaginary opponent, his feet darting. The sword gleamed in the sunlight, and the man, his eyes closed, seemed almost like he was hanging from it, the large blade whooshing through the air so forcefully.

"Are you afraid?" I asked her.

"Yes, and you?"

"Oh, sure. Last night, I was writing up some things on the computer that I want to say, and my leg kept cramping. It kills me today, like I worked out or something."

"You have, Rose-Marie, all of you have. You've been working out for a while."

Back to the confrontation. I looked down at the papers on my lap and heard thunder in the distance. My parents were seated opposite me, and Ella sat to my right. My papers shook and so did my voice as I began to speak.

Fortunate Daughter

You made me hate my body.
You made me scared of myself.
You made me think that men weren't human.
You would yell at me.
You would slap me.
You would strap me.
You tried to possess me.
You tried to own me.
You put your fingers in my vagina.
You touched my breasts.
You would look at me like you wanted to have sex with me.
You made me try and forget.
You made me feel embarrassed.
You made me ashamed.
You would watch me undress.
You made me sleep with my clothes on.
You did this for years.
You used me.
You hurt me.
You betrayed me.
You satisfied your needs through me at my expense.
You abused my trust of you.
You depended on me too much.
You made me promise not to tell.
You blamed me.
You told me I was responsible.
You would ask me if it felt good and make me tell you.
You made me sad.
You made me cry.
You made me feel guilty.
You stole my innocence.

Confrontation

You would invite me to sit next to you, so you could touch me
* sexually.*
You would ask me to kiss you.
You would ask me as if I had a choice.
You would make me go numb.
You would take me places, so you could be alone with me.
You made everyone at home hate me.
You made Mom jealous of me.
You would give me presents so I would feel special and then
* take them away if I didn't do what you wanted.*
You made me feel dirty.
You made me afraid.
Afraid to tell.
Afraid to feel.
Afraid to believe it would ever change.
Afraid to breathe at night.
Afraid to sleep in my bed.
Afraid to move.
Afraid of all men.
Afraid of all people.
Afraid of those closest to me.
Afraid of me.
Afraid to laugh.

I did my best to keep myself from faltering. Though I was reading a script, these words were mine and they were painful to hear
coming out of my mouth. I ignored any concern for my parents, or
I wouldn't have been able to speak. Both of them were crying audi-
bly, but they appeared to receive what I was saying with as much
grace as they seemed capable of. I wondered if God's love was in the
room, and I felt surprised and relieved that I wasn't crying. I'd shed
so many tears before now, perhaps I didn't need any. I struggled to

stay aware of my own response to what was happening and not get caught up in theirs.

Just at that moment, I heard Ella whisper, "You may continue."

When a man thirteen years my senior told me he was in love with me, I desperately believed him and put myself into an abusive relationship with him.

I used to stand in a crowd of people and feel unable to feel or speak.

I used to think and feel what an evil person I was all the time.

I so much did not expect anything from men that when the men I did involve myself with gave me less than what I deserved, I accepted it. I had no feeling of self-worth.

I felt the only way I could be of any value was sexually and it's a struggle for me still.

I gained weight because that was one of the only ways I thought I could protect myself.

When I am harassed on the street, I don't know how to protect myself.

When you tried to touch my body, I would spend all my energy trying to avoid you rather than tell you to leave me alone.

It is difficult to trust you today.

I would see the way you looked at me and feel confused and helpless, not knowing what to do.

I still battle with feelings of helplessness.

I feel scared every time I am vulnerable with someone.

I have to learn how to believe my lover when he tells me he loves me.

Confrontation

I don't believe I can trust him.

I felt paralyzed.

I would cover myself with layers of clothing so I could hide from you.

I constantly kept my arms folded in front of me to avoid your gaze.

I felt like I was destined to be alone.

I've had sex when I don't want to. Even with people I love. Lying there like I used to with you—feeling horrible, but not saying anything.

"Why don't we pause here?" Ella suggested. "Do either of you want to tell Rose-Marie what you hear her saying?"

I leaned back in my chair and felt relieved to take a break, but I also felt curious. My parents could be so unpredictable at times; I really didn't know where my words might have taken them.

Dad spoke first, his words flying out of his mouth like water out of a faucet. "I know I did those things. I can't take that away. I'm sorry. And I know that being sorry doesn't make any of it not true."

A deep sigh followed, and Mom, who hadn't stopped crying, went next.

"I feel like your dad," she said. "I know you and your sisters and brother were hurt. I never meant to hurt you, or have it go on so long." She let out a sound like someone was strangling her.

I wanted to comfort her, but Ella interrupted.

"It's okay. It helps that you're here and listening and taking responsibility for what happened. Many families wouldn't know how to do what you're doing now to heal." Ella was speaking matter-of-factly, but there was, as always, something soothing in her frankness and openness. They seemed calmer, and I was comforted because it was the only thing that kept me from acting on my impulse to take care of them.

"Let's continue," Ella said. "Rose-Marie would like to share with you the impact that her experience of abuse has had on her."

I knew that the hardest part was behind me. I began to feel almost elated while at the same time anguished.

I want intimacy in my life, but I never feel it.

I want to ask for help and don't.

I want to ask for love.

I want to cry and can't.

I feel unable to express any of these feelings.

I am afraid now of desire and how to express it.

I want to trust someone, but I don't feel capable.

I want to hold my feelings in, push them down and only when I am by myself do I let myself feel them.

I feel estranged from myself, feeling like there is a 'me' acting in the world and this real me somewhere else, out of reach.

I feel unsafe in the world to show my feelings.

They had stopped crying by now. There was pile of tissues bulging out of the side pocket of Mom's sweater, and Dad had torn his tissues into tiny pieces. A few of them had fallen to the floor. I noticed them as I stared at the dust motes that floated around him. I looked out the window. The clouds still looked heavy with rain about to fall.

"What do you hear Rose-Marie saying, and what can you tell her about how it makes you each feel?" Ella said. "This time, why don't you go first, Rose?"

Confrontation

"I knew it would carry on into her life. I knew it would make her life harder. I wish I could take it away. I really do." She looked right at me, and I knew she was sincere in her apology. Her words helped in a small way. "I don't feel like I had many choices other than the ones—"

"Hang on, Rose. Let's hear from you, Ned. What would you like to say?"

My father was absolutely still for a long time and then, "I understand there's no excuse for what I did. I can't say anything other than I'm sorry. I'm truly sorry for any pain I caused Rose-Marie and if I could take it away, I would."

It was quiet again. My shoulders lifted as if I were being pulled tenderly toward the ceiling. Free of gravity. My mouth was dry, and my palms were sweaty. I reached for the glass of water and took a few gulps.

We all turned to Ella and I asked, "What do we do now?"

"Well, let me just say that you've survived the most difficult part, and I'm proud of each one of you. It takes a lot of courage to do what you just did. I know that Rose-Marie wants to tell you what she wants from you now. We can do that today or schedule another time. What do you prefer, Rose-Marie?"

I felt like we had, perhaps, come far enough that day. I looked at my parents. They reminded me of those tiny little trees you find climbing up a sheer rock face on the top of a mountain—fragile, but hanging in there, nonetheless.

"We can wait, I guess. In a lot of ways, I have what I want." I knew this statement was not absolute, but it felt true. For the first time, I saw them both look somewhat natural in their response. "I'm sure we would all prefer the follow-up conversation to be here, with you by our side," I said to Ella.

For the second time that day, I felt the tension in the room lessen. My parents rose. Ella hugged Mom and shook Dad's hand.

They went out into the waiting room, and Mom asked me if they should wait.

"Sure. I just want to say goodbye to Ella." The lightness I had felt earlier was still with me. I was beginning to hope that it might be there forever.

"You should feel very pleased with yourself," Ella said, and extended her arms to me. I hugged her and relaxed in the comfort of her embrace. "Why don't you plan on coming back at your regular time, and we'll figure out our next steps together?"

"Yeah, that's fine." I turned toward the entrance and saw my parents through the glass in the front door window. Draped in sunlight, they looked small, standing there holding hands. The storm had passed us by.

2003

Reconciliation

The first American bombs were dropped on Baghdad; Martha Stewart was indicted for using privileged investment information; ex-soldier John Muhammad was found guilty of the Washington sniper shootings; and a 104-degree heat wave killed approximately 5,000 people in France.

I was at my parents' house and sitting in the dining room. The large oak table was covered with an eggshell-white paper cloth, over which was placed a second large plastic tablecloth, in case any of the children accidentally overturned their grape juice. Half-full plastic cups would be tentatively handed to them with a reminder "not to spill." But with six kids between the ages of three and twelve seated amid the adults, spills were all but inevitable.

There were fifteen people gathered at my parents' house on this warm, spring night, and the adults providentially outnumbered the children. My son, Joseph, and Anna's son, Oenghus, both nine years old and nearly seated on top of one another, gripped their drinks, more than willing to participate in a ritual that made them appear older than they were. Peter was seated beside them in his wheelchair, with Mom next to him and Dad on the other side. I was beside Dad with Isabella, Anna's daughter, and Alicia, my daughter, sitting next to me, sharing the same chair. Ben, my husband, was wedged in between them and Anna, who sat next to him on the other side. Luke, the youngest grandchild, was sitting between her and Amy, Christina's partner and one of his moms.

The center of the table was adorned with aluminum baking dishes lined with foil and filled with assorted Italian-American favorites: eggplant parmesan, manicotti with meatballs, and chicken wings smothered in a bright-red tomato sauce. There was also a salad and two or three dressings to choose from, along with containers of "sprinkle cheese," as we called it.

Before we began to eat, Mom took Dad's right hand and said, "Settle down. We're going to say a blessing and then we can eat." The rest of us, all of whom had stopped going to church years ago and most of whom seldom prayed, bowed our heads obediently, holding hands with one another, and murmured along: "Bless us, oh Lord, and these thy gifts which we are about to receive from thy bounty, through Christ, Our Lord. Amen."

Mom looked up, her white hair cut short around her small face, and smiled at my niece. "Special thanks for being able to share in the birthday celebration for Isabella!"

"Here, here," Dad said and held up his glass, filled with water. My parents didn't drink alcohol anymore, and it was a rare occasion that any of us would bring a bottle of wine. No one wanted to get buzzed around Mom and Dad. Luke hadn't stopped eating since he was placed in the highchair, and his chin and cheeks—and hair— already shimmered with red sauce. We were gathered around the table—me, my husband, Anna and her husband, Christina and her partner, and all the grandchildren.

"Papa, why are you crying?" Joseph asked.

Everyone suddenly looked at Dad, affectionately referred to as Papa by the grandkids. His eyes were wet behind his glasses. How did Joseph see that? I wondered. "Tears of gratitude, the best kind. I never would have guessed we could be together," Dad said, and motioned with his glass a second time. The boys relished the idea of clinking again. The odds of a spill increased dramatically.

"How come, Papa?" Oenghus asked.

The adults glanced at one another cursorily. It wasn't the first time we'd been given opportunity to address the difference between what we were experiencing now as compared to our own childhood years ago. Papa is a different man today than he was when we were growing up. Very different. He spoke first, and I was glad.

"I wasn't a good daddy most of the time when my own kids were young."

I was impressed. His words were brief, but honest. We hadn't completely figured out yet how to tell the kids what happened to us as children, but we all agreed we didn't want to lie about it either. That route seemed to lead to more problems for a lot of people. But the question, "What to tell?" persisted. We didn't have good role models for parenting, and the subjects of alcoholism, incest, and abuse are not easy topics for anyone to address.

"You're a good dad today," Joseph said.

I jumped in. "Yes, people can change. Papa and Nana are good to their grandchildren," I looked around, "and to all of us! We're grateful for that." The boys toasted again, spilling some of their drink.

"That's enough, boys," Ben told them, anxious they might get out of hand. "You can toast later when we have cake."

"Mom, didn't you order pizzas, too?" Christina asked, attempting to rescue her nephews from getting into trouble.

"Oh, I forgot. They're in the oven," Mom said, and her bottom rose from the chair like a hot-air balloon.

"Oh Mom, don't get up!" I bellowed, shoving a whole meatball in my mouth, before getting up from my own chair.

"You know you can't stop her from serving us," Thomas, my brother-in-law, said in a tone full of warm resignation.

I sat back down. I didn't always know how to read Thomas, especially when it came to his opinion about my parents and the impact they had on my sister, his wife. He and Amy and Ben had no idea what a ride they were going on when they married into our family. I felt an enduring respect for their willingness to support our decision to stay connected to our parents and to challenge my sisters and me when they feel like we couldn't see things clearly. Hard to do in any family, especially a family with a history of abuse.

"What are you saying about me?" Mom shouted from the kitchen as she removed two large plain-cheese pizzas from the oven. She understood our compunction to comment on her actions. We tried, even if we objected to something she did, to communicate concerns we had with affection.

"Nothing too important. We just want you with us while we eat," I said, more to myself than to her. Just the other day, Ben and my two kids, Joseph and Alicia, were asking me to sit. I was caught making the same excuses she did for being on the go.

Now, each of the kids has taken a few of Nana's meatballs and chickens wings, and they had greasy faces and fingers to prove it. That didn't stop every single one of them from standing up—some of them on their chairs—and reaching for slices of the pizza that Mom carried in. Luke was humming to himself, he was so happy, and the melodic purr could be heard during infrequent moments of quiet chewing.

"What were you playing with Auntie Rose-Marie before supper?" Anna asked Isabella.

"Auntie was laying on the couch 'cuz she was hurt, and she needed some medicine 'cuz she had a bad case of Echinacea." Isabella said, excited to report that she had taken care of me in our pretend game of nurse and patient.

"What?" Joseph and Oenghus shouted, mouths full of food. They were confused by what she told us, and they should have been.

Reconciliation

"Boys, please don't talk with food in your mouths," I said, sounding sterner than I felt.

"She means amnesia," Dad said, and we all smiled.

Isabella may have mispronounced the word, but it was an intelligent mistake. There was not a child at the table who didn't impress us with their bodies or their brains. They enjoyed one another's company and loved coming to Nana and Papa's. Granted, we didn't ever leave them unattended with my parents, and there were restrictions on Dad's physical relationship with all of them: he was not to hold them for any length of time or be alone in a room with any one of them. We came up with these guidelines as a way to feel comfortable in our visits while fostering connection with grandparents who love their grandchildren. We don't know what others would do in our boat, but this arrangement is one of the ways we've figured out how to manage our feelings and, simultaneously, not do anything to inadvertently carry out a legacy of abuse.

"I'm done," Gregory announced, climbing out of his seat. He would be four in six months and was small for his age, but very agile.

I looked to his moms to see if it was okay with them, and Anna said, "Oh, let him go. He'll be back when we have the cake, and then you can force him to eat."

"We don't have to force him," Amy said. "He loves carrots. Are there any in the salad tonight?"

"Yes." Mom winked at me and passed the bowl to her.

"So, what do we think about Pope John Paul dying?" I asked my parents amid the sounds of children talking. The phone rang. A dog barked in the yard next door.

"What's there to say?" Dad spoke first. "He's been pope for decades, spoke about a dozen languages, traveled all over the world . . . "

"I can't say I've shed any tears over the loss," Amy, my sister's wife said, with a mischievous grin. She, too, was raised Catholic and has never understood why my sisters and I were not more bitter about our religious upbringing. Mom handed out small wooden bowls. The gold necklace we gave her with miniature stick figures, representing each one of the grandchildren with their birthstone, dangled from her neck. She also gave everyone a napkin before we could tell her we didn't need one and then realize we did.

"I couldn't believe how many people flocked to Rome to pay their respects," Thomas said with a smile. We ate our iceberg lettuce salad, in the custom of Italians across the globe, at the end of our meal, one of the few cultural legacies we honored in my family—that, and hanging up pictures of the Blessed Virgin Mary. She stared down at us with pleading eyes from at least three places in this one room, and a dozen other spots around the house. I had no idea that Mom had any religious paraphernalia until I left home and came back with friends who weren't raised Catholic.

"When are we going to eat cake?" Oenghus ran back to the table and yelled out his question at the top of his lungs.

"Please do not raise your voice like that!" Amy said. "Raise it like this: 'When are we going to eat cake?'" in a high-pitched mousy voice.

"After you all finish eating and wash your hands," I said. Sometimes as the oldest sister, I can't help myself. Anna and Christina fluctuate in their ability to tolerate my bossiness, and I only hoped they didn't judge me too harshly in that moment. While the children rose as if they were in a race, the rest of us reflected more on the meaning of the pope's passing.

"At the time, the pope's visit to Boston was one of the most important days of my life," Anna said and looked at me. My sisters and I went with Dad to see him when he visited the States some twenty-four years ago. We smiled because we remembered what a physically grueling experience it was to stand there, practically nose-to-nose, for hours in the pouring rain.

Reconciliation

"What do you think today?" Amy asked, and the kids returned, frantically looking for clean paper plates.

"That we were desperate for divine intervention in our lives," I told her, and playfully threw a balled-up napkin at Peter. It hit Mom's nose instead and she giggled, rising again and going into the kitchen.

"Girls, can you clear the table and come help me?"

"I'll do that. You girls stay here with the kids," Dad said, and stood up slowly. His shoulders were stooped, his belly was too big, and his left knee was stiff. "I was digging a hole in my dream last night, and I kept hollering for you to help me," he said to Anna. She came over and stood beside him, pretending to take her imaginary shovel and dig.

"What were we looking for, Dad?" she asked good-humoredly.

"Heck if I know. Can't say I've ever been clear about what I was looking for." He sounded so sincere that I wondered, not for the first time, how he made sense of his life. I was forty years old and I still didn't really know; but I did know he lived in a constant state of gratitude and guilt.

"I help you, Papa," Alicia came over and hugged his leg. He patted her head until she released his leg and walked into the kitchen. However much he enjoys these moments, we don't experience them with the ease of a family that has no history of abuse. We are grateful that the grandchildren have good relationships with their grandparents, but it is with painstaking deliberation that my sisters and I, along with our partners, make the daily decision to be in my parents' lives the way we are. The rock thrown into the pond of our childhood has never stopped making ripples, and we always have the choice to walk away completely. But for the most part, we haven't wanted to leave our family, our connection to one another, our place of origin. Both of my parents took full responsibility for their offenses, and my father learned to regulate his abusive behaviors.

"Is there any ice cream?" Isabella asked.

"Nope, we didn't have time to get any," Mom said, winking at all of us, returning with a tray of Neapolitan ice cream, sherbet, and chocolate sorbet.

"That coffee smells good, Mom. Is it decaf?" I asked. "I don't want to be up too late tonight."

"You betcha; I don't want you losing sleep over something I did," Mom said and winked.

"I want strawberry!" Isabella yelled, and Mom stood up and said, "Everyone who wants dessert in honor of Isabella's birthday needs to go do the hokey pokey with Auntie Christina in the living room." Christina looked up, surprised by the idea, but immediately ran into the living room, wiggling her hips and motioning for the kids to form a circle. Mom left the room and returned to the table with one of the prettiest pink-frosted, orange-flower-covered chocolate cakes I'd ever seen. The top of it was so bright, it glistened in the light of four fat candles!

"My cake is here!" Isabella yelled. The adults stood around the table as the kids scrambled to get a seat. Gregory and Alicia argued over who should sit next to Isabella.

"No fighting," Peter said, and reached for Alicia so she could sit on his lap.

"Where's Nana?" I asked.

"I'm coming. I just wanted to—" Before she finished, we heard it. "Happy Birthday" sung by a man with a surprisingly solemn alto blasting out of my parents' stereo. We joined in and smiled as Isabella sat, her face hovering over the cake. Four candles glowing in the now muted light of day's ending.

Epilogue

Mom looks small in the oversized La-Z-Boy, her short bony legs not reaching the floor, slippers dangling off her toes. I hand her pages I've selected from my manuscript, this memoir. I wonder how hard it will be for her to read them. I don't want to hurt her. She is in her seventies, and our relationship is in a solid place, but it is longstanding and delicate. Like palimpsest, those parchment papers used more than once, the old ink scraped off to allow new words and images to be inscribed. Invariably, the erasure is incomplete, and remnants of the earlier text endure.

"Do you want me to tell you something more about what I am asking you to read?" I ask.

"No, just give it to me."

"Okay." I stand beside her. I feel adrift and mixed up, but hand her the pages titled Chapter Two.

"Do you want to go somewhere else?" She looks up at me, over her bifocals, and smiles with affection.

"Where?" I feel suddenly like a child, wanting to please her by doing what she tells me.

"I don't know. You're a writer. Why don't you go practice your craft?" she asks and winks, picking up the pencil I left on the end table beside her.

I turn toward my study. I decide if I can't write, then I can at least check my email. I crave knowing if my mom understands how compelled I feel to share this story.

In less time than I think necessary, she finishes reading the excerpt, the only section of the book that describes my family before I was born, as pertinent to my fate as the days thereafter.

"You can come back," she says in a quiet voice.

Is she done? Did I upset her? Will she want to talk with me? Why should I care how she feels? But part of coming out the other side means that I *am* concerned about her and Dad's well-being. They stopped being my enemies a long time ago, when they took responsibility for their offenses, and my father learned to control his abusive behaviors.

I pull over a chair and sit next to her. She shuffles the papers on her lap and asks, "How do you want to do this? I know you must have some *way* of doing this."

"Why don't you just talk, and I'll listen? For others that I've shared my writing with, I find if I comment while someone is giving me feedback, it makes it hard for the person to communicate to me what they really think."

"Oh, you know me, quivering in my boots," she says and smiles again. I know it's going to be all right, and I breathe a big sigh.

"You know what I mean, Ma. This is not easy stuff to read."

"I lived through it. How could reading about it be worse?"

"You'd be surprised. I'll make us some coffee first."

"Are there more pages?" She yells into the kitchen, as I look for the Sanka she brought with her and left at my home the last time she visited. She has always preferred instant over percolated, claiming it tastes better.

"Yes, this is one of the nineteen chapters I've written."

"I want to read more."

I sigh again and feel even lighter. That is what all writers want to hear. I wanted to hear that from Mom but couldn't assume that was possible. I bring her a cup of coffee, in a mug that is easy for her to hold in her little hands. I sit down beside her again as she begins her review.

Epilogue

"You'll need to change the names of the people and the places if you want my permission to go ahead and get this book published." She winks at me through her glasses.

She then peers over each page, occasionally saying, "You got that right" or "That date may not be accurate." I tell her I'll get help from people who know more than I do, when the time comes.

I don't know what I'm expecting, until I realize it's not coming. She's not going to say how she feels. She's not even acting like it makes her feel anything. Is she trying to protect me? Does she not have any feelings? Should I ask? It's hard for me to know what her experience has been, what it's taught her. It always has been.

I let her share the way in which she is most comfortable; it's for her that I listen, page by page. I'm relieved she's sitting next to me in my home. I am grateful she is alive to give me her blessing. We're comfortable with one another.

After lunch, which she'll make for me, we'll watch half an old movie on a DVD, nap, and then my children will come home. The kids love their nana. They love both their grandparents, Nana and Papa. Papa—my dad—hasn't read the book, either. I don't think he wants to read it. He hasn't asked. But that's not the only reason. He doesn't ask for anything.

A few months back, I had invited my whole family to a therapy session. We sat with Ella, our family therapist from way back, in one of the half-dozen offices where we'd sat with her before. My sister Christina and her partner, Amy, were there and both my parents and me. My other sister, Anna, her husband, my own husband, and my brother didn't come, each one for different reasons.

"I'm really thankful you're all here, and I appreciate your willingness to understand what it is I'm trying to do." I felt both relief and surprise, confident about my intentions, unafraid of what might happen. I hadn't always felt this way. Ella's presence needed no explanation. She helped me confront both my parents about the abuse I suffered as a child and teenager, over twenty years ago. At the time, I truly believed the process would kill my father, literally. I felt that same fear letting Mom read the pages from my book.

Ella looked older, rounder, but beautiful and poised, the way I remembered her. She explained to the group, "Assuming that you all understand our purpose in being together, why don't you each take turns sharing what you feel about Rose-Marie's aspiration, her determination to publish." She looked at me and then said, "Communicate any fears you have about what that means."

My mom started off by saying, "The world is not a forgiving place." We nodded in agreement; I'm sure each one of us wished that was not the case. "I worry about people, mostly strangers, finding out things about us I don't want them to know, I've never wanted them to know."

I felt immediately frustrated, hearing her speak. Her anxiety hit dead on one of my main motivations to share this story. Cultural assumptions besiege any and all conversations about sexual abuse, perpetrators, and victims. I wondered again if sexual abuse of a child by an adult, one who loves you, is possibly the worst offense a person can commit, then why is it so common? Our society has yet to figure out how to prevent sexual abuse.

My dad, his nearly bald head in need of a haircut, reacted to Ella's question by saying, "The way you talk about the book makes me interested in it, more than I thought I would." He went on to say that my description of the book prompted him to imagine someone approaching him to ask about his role, indicating that he could somehow use it as a teachable moment. He didn't seem scared, more curious than anything. Not that it would have surprised me if he did feel afraid. Not that he couldn't feel afraid of the story's implications, but his emotions were difficult for me to read; they're opaque.

My sister Christina added, "I think we have to have a little faith

Epilogue

in Rose-Marie and let go of what we can't predict about the future."
She laughed nervously, and I realized she was also more uncomfortable than she initially let on. "It's just a story, Rosie's story, not ours.
If the best thing happens and it's published, it might be a big deal
for a little while, and then something else will come along to grab
people's attention."

Her partner, my sister-in-law Amy, followed. "I'm concerned
about my kids, all our kids." She was referring to the grandchildren,
six of them; whatever they may or may not have understood about
why they couldn't be at Nana and Papa's home unsupervised hasn't
seemed to deter them from developing a deep connection to both
my parents. A safe connection. Their grandparents loved the children, and in turn the children loved them back. And the legacy of
abuse had stopped.

Together, we considered what the kids might grasp already and
the possibility that my story's publication would undoubtedly have
an impact. Did I want that sort of renown for any of us?

I felt disappointed that my sister Anna hadn't joined us. I
wanted her to feel less threatened by my book, or by her perception
of it. Historically, we've given one another plenty of room to answer
back to our past the way we wanted. This book was my choice, not
anyone else's.

"I have fears," I told my gathered family. "I don't know what
is going to happen when people read this story. I do not want to
hurt any of you, expose you unnecessarily to public recrimination.
I realize we wouldn't be here today if it weren't for the work we did.
I trust our family's ability to remain connected through the aftermath of this story getting told."

Why shouldn't I? We are where we are against the odds, actively
connected to one another. It's why Mom is with me, and why I gave
her the pages I just shared with you.

"Hope is both the earliest and the most indispensable virtue inherent in the state of being alive. If life is to be sustained, hope must remain, even where confidence is wounded, trust impaired."

—Erik H. Erikson

Afterword

ealing from childhood sexual abuse and remaining connected to one's family as I did is not an option for many people. I understand that. Healing can, and often must, occur only by leaving one's family, but at a cost, always at a cost. Insofar as my parents took full responsibility for their wrongdoings and participated in a formal confrontation process orchestrated by experts in interpersonal sexual abuse, I was allowed an exceptional healing opportunity. However unusual that might be, my recovery is real, and I wish to share it.

If the abuse were still occurring or had yet to be openly addressed, the choice I made to stay in relationship with my family and my father, the perpetrator of the abuse, would not have been viable. Of this, I am certain. In families where this is true, victims of abuse generally pretend nothing ever happened (at their own peril) or leave so as to not to live a lie and become whole again.

I still question why my story is virtually unknown, or when I share it with friends and colleagues, I am often met with raised eyebrows or even veiled hostility. What is our investment in believing that once a victim, always a victim, once a perpetrator, always a perpetrator? That people who do bad things, are not capable of doing good? That no treatment works to stop sexual abuse, let alone allows for the option of victim and perpetrator to come together in a process that ends the cycle of sexual abuse? Why can't I find my story anywhere else? It seems to me that our culture is invested in the belief that the perpetrator is evil and beyond reform. We also accept as true that once a victim, always a victim.

I've listened to Desmond Tutu in The Forgiveness Project and his words ring true in my life. Maybe they do in yours.

Granting forgiveness to my mother and father—and everyone who could have helped and chose not to—allowed me to experience more transformation in my life. If I had chosen not to forgive, most people would understand, relate, and support me. But I would be less free.

My life is filled with things that most people wouldn't believe a person with my background could have, including meaningful work, a partner whose love sustains me, children who are thriving, a community of kind friends, and a garden that blooms every year. I have questions about my life still and why it is that I feel like a whole and unbroken person, despite my injuries. But the path I have walked, while not easy, has resulted in my being the person I am today, and I am glad to be who I am.

It is also important to remember that when childhood sexual abuse happens in one's family, no person in that family escapes the impact or the consequences of such a violation, even if they were not personally abused. They, too, are made to feel unsafe and helpless.

I did my best not to speak for anyone else in my family, but I welcome the telling of stories of other family members, bystanders, so to speak. We have much to learn still about the experience they have of feeling dominated by fear and abuse even if they, themselves, were not the main target of abuse. We have more to learn about victimhood and survivorhood, especially as it relates to sexual trauma. We have more to learn about the relationship between reparation and justice, true justice.

Because I have let go of my anger and resentment, I can feel curious, safe, and confident, attributes that people who have not let go of their rage seem limited in their ability to feel. Again, if sharing

Afterword

my story makes it more possible for others to restore themselves and feel less alone, then I feel obliged to share it. I am a healer—albeit a wounded one—using and sharing my understanding of then to better understand now.

I have wondered for many years about the impact on those of us who have come out on the other side, scathed but strong. I feel a part of a community that has been denied a public voice and even knowledge of ourselves as a community. I want this story to become part of the solution, adding to the national dialogue on how to "restore justice" in a family riddled with childhood abuse and sexual trauma and awash in the alcoholism that often instigates them.

There is a mechanism in people that stops us from talking about bad experiences and makes us reluctant to stir up the past. But secrets have the tendency to foster a specific version of reality in which the individual pieces must be arranged so neatly that if just one were to change position, the whole picture would fall apart. Most everyone, but certainly people with abuse histories, return to painful events and search their memories, examine them, attempting to come to terms with their past, appreciating that the past—like the future—is not over.

Memories are essential and helpful in understanding who we are but should not be viewed as the last word or a factual account, regardless of how precise or abundant they seem. They are selective, especially when it comes to which incidences we hold onto in the first place. How we understand them requires us to delve into a world filled with holes, with questions that, at the time they occurred, might not have been asked, at least not out loud. That is why in families, we argue over what should be remembered and what should be forgotten.

I call this book a memoir. It reflects a reconstruction based on my best recollection, and I have chosen to write about certain events using multiple memories stemming from these recollections. Not only does this form of remembrance reveal something that has been true in my life, it might well explain the way you understand your own layered, contradictory, multifaceted past.

Acknowledgments

Writing this book was demanding of my time, my energy, my integrity, and my faith. I could not have done it without my husband. He has never once doubted the value of this story and my need to tell it. That is true love.

Deep gratitude to the brave and dedicated feminists, who were the first mental health practitioners in my life to convince me that it's not enough to just survive.

I'm grateful to Beth Fraster for her tireless and exuberant support. She shares my belief that it is through the pursuit of healing and reconciliation that we cultivate healthier societies and free ourselves from trauma, violence, and oppression.

To the facilitators of writing groups I took part in, who provided space for courage and taught me that writing need not be a solitary act: Dori Ostermiller of Writers In Progress, Janine Roberts, Sally Bellerose, Linda McCullough Moore, and Carol Edelstein & Robert Barber.

A very special thanks to various editors in my journey towards publication: David King, Libby Maxey, Vernon David, Paula Stacey, and Fran Fahey. With their critical eyes and coaxing, I became a better writer.

To She Writes Press, for believing in my story and making it possible for me to get my book out into the world—a place in great need of transformation.

Fortunate Daughter

To my friends, who acted as readers, giving of their time and assessment, especially Jimmy Grogan, Helen Tuohy, Matthew Detroy, Amy Grunder, Bram Gunther, and Debra Granik. Your thoughtful and unfeigned responses urged me along.

To my family of origin. My grandparents for their tenacity. My parents for their bravery. My siblings for their fierce companionship and hilarity. My nibblings for the joy I've felt in watching who they have become. And my children, for all the ways they teach me to be my whole self and inspire me to remain curious and compassionate.

Lastly, to nature. Her beauty and complexity reminds me that I am not alone. Ever.

About the Author

Photo credit: Jason Threlfall

Rosie McMahan was brought up in Somerville, MA, at a time when kids and dogs roamed the streets in unlawful packs and the walk to a barroom or Catholic church was less than a quarter of a mile in any direction. She and her husband moved to western Massachusetts in 2001 to raise their children.

Rosie's writing has received prizes and she can be seen reading in local venues, including Pecha Kucha (a local storytelling event), the annual Garlic & Arts Festival, and the Greenfield Annual Word Festival (GAWF). She has also been published in several journals, including *Silkworm*, *Typehouse Literary Magazine*, *Black Fox Literary Magazine*, the 2017 *Gallery of Readers Anthology*, and *Passager Journal*. She currently lives in Amherst, MA, and runs a private practice called Optimistic Options.

SELECTED TITLES FROM SHE WRITES PRESS

She Writes Press is an independent publishing company
founded to serve women writers everywhere.
Visit us at www.shewritespress.com.

Raising Myself: A Memoir of Neglect, Shame, and Growing Up Too Soon by Beverly Engel. $16.95, 978-1-63152-367-0. A powerfully inspiring and unflinchingly honest story of how best-selling author and abuse recovery expert Beverly Engel made her way in the world—in spite of her mother's neglect and constant criticism, undergoing sexual abuse at nine, and being raped at twelve.

Secrets in Big Sky Country: A Memoir by Mandy Smith. $16.95, 978-1-63152-814-9. A bold and unvarnished memoir about the shattering consequences of familial sexual abuse—and the strength it takes to overcome them.

Fourteen: A Daughter's Memoir of Adventure, Sailing, and Survival by Leslie Johansen Nack. $16.95, 978-1-63152-941-2. A coming-of-age adventure story about a young girl who comes into her own power, fights back against abuse, becomes an accomplished sailor, and falls in love with the ocean and the natural world.

Say It Out Loud: Revealing and Healing the Scars of Sexual Abuse by Roberta Dolan. $16.95, 978-1-938314-99-5. An in-depth guide to healing the wounds caused by sexual abuse, written by a survivor who's lived the process firsthand.

Baffled by Love: Stories of the Lasting Impact of Childhood Trauma Inflicted by Loved Ones by Laurie Kahn. $16.95, 978-1-63152-226-0. For three decades, Laurie Kahn has treated clients who were abused as children—people who were injured by someone who professed to love them. Here, she shares stories from her own rocky childhood along with those of her clients, weaving a textured tale of the all-too-human search for the "good kind of love."

Singing with the Sirens: Overcoming the Long-Term Effects of Childhood Sexual Exploitation by Ellyn Bell and Stacey Bell. $16.95, 978-1-63152-936-8. With metaphors of sea creatures and the force of the ocean as a backdrop, this work addresses the problems of sexual abuse and exploitation of young girls, taking the reader on a poetic journey toward finding healing from within.